The Radiance Technique®
and
The Animal Kingdom

D1596381

COPUBLISHERS:
Radiance Associates &
Radiance Stress Management International, Inc.

The Radiance Technique®
and
The Animal Kingdom

by
Marvelle Lightfields

Radiance Associates   St. Petersburg, Florida

First Printing, June 1992

First Edition © 1992 by Marvelle Lightfields

Library of Congress Catalog Card Number 92-60782

ISBN 0-933267-04-5

Printed in the United States of America

CONTENTS

INTRODUCTION

What an exciting moment this is in the ongoing and historic evolution of The Radiance Technique®! We are sharing this dynamic and joyous part of our lives which includes our animal friends. Many of you have been waiting for this book to be published because you know the journey of inner-connection that you've found with animals through applying The Radiance Technique® yourself. The sharing of the universal, radiant energy of The Radiance Technique® with the animals in my world has become a natural part of my life. My bonds of love have grown deeper with the animals I know on the outer planes, who share my home, and with the whole animal kingdom as I have used The Radiance Technique® to assist different members of the animal kingdom and those species nearing extinction.

I would like to express my deep gratitude to Dr. Barbara Ray who has protected this science of universal, transcendental, radiant energy. As the founder of The Radiance Technique Association International, Inc. and the one person entrusted with deeper, inner knowledge of the science of all seven degrees—the keys of the science—she opened the gateways for all of us to follow her in the use and expansion of The Radiance Technique. She has kept intact the authentic science and brought it into the daily lives of people everywhere. She has trained Authorized Instructors to teach others and she has trained students in all seven of the degrees.

Her work with the technique and her training of others in it has encircled the globe. Most of her service remains unseen, yet it is ongoing and of such a generous nature that many people who never realize the depth of her efforts in the outer dimensions still *feel* the warmth and heart-expanding support in their lives. A world traveler with a special devotion to expanding awareness of our "inner-Radiant-connection" to all life, she has spent extended time working with Inner Light at a number of natural power centers on Planet Earth and continues with her dedication to expanding our natural bonds with the unique and precious animal kingdom on earth.

She founded The Radiance Technique Association International, Inc., for students to learn more about the technique, through their sharings and contact with one another, through education and publications, and to link members everywhere in a worldwide network of Light-energy. Beginning in 1979 with her own teaching and writing, she published the first book ever written on the subject—the first edition of *The 'Reiki' Factor in The Radiance Technique®* in 1980. Now a dozen years later, we are able to see the impact of such sustaining and stabilizing actions. She had the vision to see that in the future students everywhere would be exploring and discovering the daily uses of this technique. She saw the natural unfolding of using radiant energy with animals and she supported the publication of a book about it years before it actually manifested. In her own pioneering book, she wrote movingly of using the technique with animals and plants. She has given us permission to use that chapter in this publication so that more people can read it. We are honored to share it as Chapter 2, reprinted from *The 'Reiki' Factor in The Radiance Technique®* by Dr. Barbara Ray.

Dr. Barbara Ray has been my guide, my teacher and my inspiration. Without her this book would never have been begun and certainly would never have been completed and published. In addition, her loving support has touched hundreds of students worldwide who have written to us for inclusion in the book. This book is dedicated to her with deepest honoring and gratitude for my being given the joyous opportunity to have the experience of using The Radiance Technique® with myself, with others, with plants and all of nature... and especially with my own animal friends, and with members of the animal kingdom wherever they may be.

If you have never shared radiant energy with members of the animal kingdom, this book will open many gateways of service and support for you. You will find examples and sharings from people all over the globe who are participating daily in radiant support of animals. This book is full of smiles and love, and in it are some of the real tears of tenderness that come from profound experiences. It is radiantly alive with sharings that have expanded me and I know will expand you!

There have been so many people who helped make this book possible because of what they have naturally and spontaneously done—using The Radiance Technique® with animals in situations we might never have thought about! This radiant, harmless, supportive energy has been the key to their creativity and their discovery process. I am filled with gratitude for the learning I have gained and for the experience of joy and laughter that has been part of the process of bringing these sharings together. This book is about the deepening relationship that can be shared between human and animal as we walk in harmony on Planet Earth aware of our bond with all that is alive.

In her extensive and inspiring book on transcendental energy that Dr. Barbara Ray published in 1988 called *The Expanded Reference Manual of The Radiance Technique®*, she wrote deeply of the joys that can be discovered with this technique for accessing radiant, loving energy by the one who truly uses it for all Life. In her section on "Animals", she wrote:

> One of the greatest joys is using The Radiance Technique® with animals and pets of all kinds. All animals respond each in its own way from within when contacted with this radiance. When possible the hands-on application usually allows for a special radiant energy bond between you and the pet. When the hands-on application is not possible or appropriate such as with untamed or wild animals, you would need to learn the use of The Second Degree or beyond to access, activate and direct this radiant energy. On the living planet Earth there are many kingdoms all in an unfolding process. What a profound opportunity for supporting and "inner-connecting" with the animal kingdom in its journey to Light. We are ALL, in our True Inner Light, one essence. For a more extensive discussion with specific data, see Chapter 12, "Pets, Plants and The Radiance Technique®," *The 'Reiki' Factor in The Radiance Technique,®* by Barbara Ray, Ph.D. See also: BIRDS, CATS, DOGS, HORSES, PLANTS, NATURE, RELAXATION.

Please know that you are in these pages, too, even if you have not yet written to us or your sharing is not included in this particular edition. Our real interconnection runs deeply through our inner plane network. This book is a continuum from the past, through the present, into and through the future. It is presented as a beginning with the express direction of continuing over the years to publish more about The Radiance Technique® and animals.

As the sharings were compiled and I began the writing of this book, I became more deeply aware of how trusting and Real are the ones who live in the animal kingdom. Where we might question, they simply respond. Where we might hesitate, they come toward radiant energy as plants grow toward the sun. Animals have a natural interaction with universal energy; it is a direct and loving experience for them. In this book, you will find many natural ways to grow in your interactions with animals. The purpose of this book is to bring you together with others who have shared the radiance, joy and love of universal energy with their animal friends worldwide and to help our circle grow!

Marvelle Lightfields
January, 1992

A SPECIAL READER'S NOTE: Throughout this book you will notice that we sometimes use The Radiance Technique® which includes the correct "R" delineating it as a registered service mark. This mark is registered for the use of The Radiance Technique Association International, Inc. and for Authorized Instructors. It denotes this authentic technique and no other. Its use in books such as this is to refer to the actual and authentic technique itself and no others. Sometimes, in this book we have used the words without the registry mark which is correct for us to do since we have previously introduced it properly. We have also used TRT to stand for this service marked phrase whenever it was more appropriate to do so.

READERS' NOTE

You will notice many references throughout this book to the book by Dr. Barbara Ray, *The Expanded Reference Manual of The Radiance Technique®*. This important addition to the information used by students of TRT worldwide is a complete A-to-Z of the uses of radiant, universal energy. It is, therefore, extremely beneficial and informative for people who have never studied The Radiance Technique® but are interested in knowing more about accessing and using universal energy. There are over 600 entries and over 75,000 words expressing the everyday uses of universal energy for exploration and personal development. You are invited to read it whether or not you have studied The Radiance Technique®. Please refer to the resources in the Addresses section for more information on how to get it.

A portion of the sales from each copy of *The Radiance Technique® and The Animal Kingdom* is being donated to The Radiance Technique Association International, Inc. and/or The Radiance Foundation, Inc.

EDITOR'S NOTE: All Authorized Instructors of The Radiance Technique® are certified by Radiance Stress Management International, Inc., and recognized by The Radiance Technique Association International, Inc. Please see Addresses Page for where to direct your inquiries.

CHAPTER ONE

THE RADIANCE TECHNIQUE® AND ANIMALS AROUND THE WORLD

One of the most joyous discoveries for you as a student of The Radiance Technique® is that you will use each degree that you learn with your animal friends. There are no limitations to the sharing of universal, radiant, and sustaining energy with members of the kingdom of animals. As you learned in your very first class for The First Degree, The Radiance Technique® is harmless and beneficial, and may be used with animals, plants and any living energy system.

Dr. Barbara Ray has written in *The 'Reiki' Factor in The Radiance Technique,*® in Chapter 12, about the use of universal energy with animals and plants. We have received her permission to reprint that chapter in full as this book's Chapter 2. In the chapter are profound sharings from students and from Dr. Ray herself. She reminds us that "Animals and plants are an integral part of our planetary system, and their destiny is linked with ours." Many students of The Radiance Technique have discovered for themselves this important "inner" connection with animals, discovering ways to use radiant energy to support and honor animals whether as friends in the home, or as friends in the wild.

This honoring of the differences between humans and animals is a vital part of bonding with the natural world in our lives. We are exceptionally fortunate to be able to invite specific animals to share our homes with us. And in this shared life, the practical applications are limitless. However, there is a natural relationship within the animal kingdom itself that needs to be honored. Animals are not humans, even though we

1

coexist very well together. We need to remember that we bear the greater responsibility. We are their caretakers.

Using The Radiance Technique® in your relationship with animals is profound and just plain fun as well. As you use radiant energy you are helping the pet or animal in many different ways. In *The Expanded Reference Manual of The Radiance Technique,*® Dr. Ray has shared the entry "helping" on page 50 as follows:

> "Throughout our lives we often find ourselves in situations where we have the opportunity to help ourselves, someone else and/or pets, animals and plants. Sometimes we feel helpless or even powerless. You can use TRT for helping anytime, anyplace and in any situation. The Radiance Technique is completely *safe*, easy to learn and can be taught to children. It is one of the most effective self-help techniques available in modern times."

Reprinted with permission
Copyright © 1987 Barbara Ray

Throughout this book you will find sharings of those who have helped their pets or other animals, creating deepening bonds of friendship and relationship. Even though the relationship with larger animals such as horses, mules, cows and other large animals involves the animal remaining outdoors, students using The Radiance Technique® have reported a fuller bonding that "goes beyond" anything they knew before. Many people train or educate these larger domestic animals to respond to do certain tasks. How wonderful to be able to use The Radiance Technique® as part of the communication process.

Following is a sharing about using TRT with some of the larger animals:

> "I have been working especially with cows on the inner planes. In England we have a cow disease called scrapey or 'mad cow disease' which has affected large numbers of animals and has been passed by man's lack of care in supplying foodstuffs. I have been tuning in with these cows for a long time and working with the energy of GRATITUDE for their support of their human family through the supply of milk and meat. I am continually experiencing my inner-connection with them in my use of

The Radiance Technique® hands-on, feeling them moving through my heart centre and expanding my heart centre."

Ingrid St. Clare
The Fifth Degree
England

A veterinarian with a practice in the state of New York, offers another view of interacting with larger animals:

"On the Sunday that I had just finished taking The Second Degree seminar, I was called to attend a horse with a very severe colic condition. Colic is the worst, the No. 1 killer of horses.

"I went up to the horse and started checking her over. She was in such extreme, severe pain, it was unbelievable. She was in severe shock. She was totally wet with sweating from the pain and the shock. She had absolutely no muscle tone. She just kept rolling from side to side, trying to stand up. Her eyes were glazed and her abdomen was completely distended–to nearly twice the size of what it should be. Respiration was way up as was her heart rate–again, from the shock.

"Then I remembered what I had learned that day in The Second Degree. I put my hand on the horse's side where the rib cage and flank meet. And the minute I did, there was a surge of energy that just flushed through me and the horse. And the horse picked up her head, turned around, looked me directly in the eyes, and, I swear, seemed to say, 'Well, you've been here five minutes. What took you so long?'

"I held my two hands there on her sides and used the Cosmic Symbols I had learned at The Second Degree and I could feel the loops of intestines that were so spastic and so painful underneath the ribs relaxing and letting go. It's amazing that I could feel all this through that tissue.

"Within 10 minutes or less, the horse began to release great volumes of gas from both ends. I continued with this energy balancing for another 10 minutes, and every two or three minutes the horse would release more gas.

"You just had to be there to feel the change in this animal. The animal was completely transformed and healthy. I could barely believe what I had been part of."

Dr. Patrick Tersigni
The Third Degree
New York

Many alumni of The Radiance Technique® also train their birds, dogs or cats as well, helping them to grow and learn, spending valuable time with them in a communication process that goes beyond "commands." (See Chapter 8.)

From the sharings we have compiled, we have learned even more deeply that the opportunity for communication is not limited to a particular species, a certain location or to smaller animals in the home; gentle creatures of the sea also respond to radiant energy in loving and trusting interactions with humans. Here is one of the many sharings that describe the deepening of such awareness:

"I work aboard cargo ships in the Trans-Pacific trade, crossing the Pacific Ocean every three weeks from Japan to California with big loads.

"This year I have encountered more sea and sky creatures than before. Birds of all kinds–sea hawks, owls, exotic species and even homing pigeons. Some are curious, some want to rest a little while, and some wish to stow-away.

"Whenever whales are spotted ahead, I try to avoid colliding with them by changing course. But, recently a whale went out of its way to approach closely to the vessel and swim alongside just the way the dolphins do. I have never been this close to one in the open sea. I wanted to reach out and pat it.

"These are special occasions to direct universal energy to all these beings, and when it happens, I experience a thoughtless, wordless transcendence whenever I can share The Radiance Technique."

Howard Gay
The Third Degree (3A)
United States Merchant Marines
Hong Kong

There is such a unity of expression when alumni share the harmless, universal energy of TRT. Here is a sharing from Hawaii that also expresses the awareness of that deep inner bond and contact:

"I had been asked to give The Radiance Technique to Echo, that is the name of the dog. The owner told me that he was very old and there were so many things wrong with him that he could not be well again.

4

"While I was sharing energy with him, he became more and more relaxed. I put my hand on his outer hip–he raised his leg without any suggestion from me in any way, then I was able to put my other hand on the inside of his leg. For the time my hands were there, he kept his leg in the air. When I needed him to turn over, I barely touched him and he rolled over. The owner of this dog was watching the entire time. She was so amazed at the response of her dog. She said: 'One can never turn him over–he just cannot do it.'

"My hands went three times to his thyroid glands. I wondered why. At the end of the session the owner said that she forgot to tell me that he has a thyroid problem too.

"I touched his face to say goodbye–he looked at me and his eyes were filled with gratitude. He followed me to the car without limping at all. He was severely limping before the session.

"In silence my inner observation during the session with him was that we were one. And it was wonderful!"

Deva Magdalena
The Third Degree (3A)
Hawaii

Within this book, we have selected sharings from people around the globe who have interacted with animals using The Radiance Technique® with domesticated or tame animals, as well as with wild animals. Usually the wild animals cannot be touched so many of those experiences involve students who have studied The Second Degree or beyond. Even animals in zoos that no longer live in the wild have had interactions with alumni using The Radiance Technique® without actual touch. (See Chapter 4.)

BEGINNING WITH HANDS-ON

Let us begin, however, with the radiant touch of the hands-on process with animals, specifically domestic animals that live with or near humans. In The First Degree you received an Official Handbook for The Radiance Technique® that has a specific section dedicated to hands-on with animals. To expand on that, we would like also to remind you of all the many references within *The Expanded Reference Manual of The*

Radiance Technique® that give support to your interactions with birds, dogs, cats, horses and animals of all kinds.

Whether you are a beginner or have used radiant and universal energy for some time, you can always expand your interactions. Time spent on hands-on with your animal friend may vary from day to day, from just a few minutes to an hour or more. However, don't wait for a crisis, a disease, or a need at the physical level to begin using hands-on as part of the bonding with the animal. As Dr. Ray writes in the next chapter, developing a regular pattern of hands-on sessions with animals supports, builds and maintains their health and well-being before any emergency ever occurs. That health maintenance is as important to animals as it is to humans for they share our contemporary stresses by being involved with us.

Especially important is the arrival of a new animal or young animal into your household. Through petting, stroking and hands-on, you begin a loving process that deepens your relationship with your new friend.

All animals that are sharing living space with humans need touch as part of their relationship. Many veterinarians suggest that having an animal learn to eat from your hand is an important part of the health care relationship that you wish to establish. If ever you need to administer medication, you will want to be able to have the animal take it from you and your hands without feeling threatened. Also the more you touch your animal and look at it, the more you will naturally notice when it needs medical or other support for illness or accident. Even tooth loss which seems to occur especially in older cats and dogs can be prevented if the caretaker begins a regular program of tooth and gum massage when the animal is still a baby and continues with such things as special brushes and toothpaste especially formulated for the animal as the young animal becomes used to this touching as a regular part of the daily grooming process.

In actually applying hands-on, always use a light touch, beginning with the petting and stroking process. Your hands have been activated as part of your very first seminar for The Radiance Technique. You are accessing and directing universal, harmless energy as you pet and stroke the animal. An important reminder is that most animals use their eyes as part of their defense process in life and you would never place your hands over their eyes.

6

Animals also have a radiant energy field and you are inter-connecting universal energy that you are accessing with your activated hands with their centers of energy. It is never necessary to "cover" a specific part of the body of an animal if it is sensitive (such as the eyes) or if it is injured. Any injured part of the body receives the benefit of the whole hands-on process since the animal is also a whole system, just as you are.

When animals are in a restful cycle, they will usually allow your hands to rest a while in one position. However, let them be your guide. They know if it is time for activity or time for rest and their "mind" doesn't contradict them. Begin gradually and expand the amount of time with this hands-on process, letting the animal become more used to your hands touching them. Radiant touch becomes a natural part of the cuddling and petting that you do with them. There is never a reason to force or to pursue the animal for a hands-on session. These bonding times develop and grow and often become a favorite time to be together spontaneously.

USING RADIANT ENERGY—EVERYDAY OF YOUR LIFE!

Sometimes the animal even "helps" you with its awareness and response as in this sharing:

"The Radiance Technique® has become so much a part of my life that I don't know where it begins or ends. Amazingly enough, since I am analytical to a fault, I no longer try to determine the energy's boundaries. What I had not realized, however, was how much a part of my cat's life The Radiance Technique has become.

"Foozi is basically still a kitten and touching her stomach or paws is an open invitation to be bitten. This has, of course, made me determined to do so and escape unscathed, but even when she's soundly asleep, the slightest touch of those forbidden areas brings her awake and attacking. This has become a game now, so I was concerned when I had her spayed and declawed.

"The day I brought her home from the vet's, she was sore, unhappy and still stressed from her ordeal. The only way I could help was with The Radiance Technique, but since I can't touch her stomach and her paws in the best of times, I contented myself with placing my hands on her side.

7

"A few seconds later, one eye opened and stared at me and I thought, uh oh, here it comes. The next thing I knew, Foozi rolled over on her side and my hands slid to her stomach, right over the incision. I was surprised when she just stretched out and started purring, but I was stunned at what happened next.

"She rearranged herself slightly and slid her paws under my hands! And so we sat for about an hour and a half. Three times a day for the next four days we went through the same routine. In spite of the fact that she took a dislike to the stitches and pulled them out the day after she came home, Foozi healed quickly and well, and is now back to her normal self, which means I am once again not allowed to touch tummy or paws."

Penney D'Ascoli
The Second Degree
Florida

You can also use your hands to add a radiant energy support just beyond the level of touch as the animal is asleep or nearby. The Radiance Technique® accesses universal energy and your hands interact with the energy field of the animal 1 to 2 inches above the level of touch.

Explore beginning a Heart Meld this way with yourself and your friend, even when touch is not yet possible. You can place one hand on your own heart and extend the other hand to embrace the energy field near the animal's heart. You can expand and deepen the joy of this bonding using touch as you meld the loving energy of your heart with their heart, when touch becomes your natural way of being together. We have many sharings in this book that include heart expanding times with animals in the loving energy of The Radiance Technique.®

USING RADIANT TOUCH WITH DIFFERENT ANIMALS

Animal lovers often have several animals in their immediate family, giving them abundant opportunities for use of The Radiance Technique. Here are some valuable insights into crisis support and discovery with the methods of hands-on and directing energy to different animals:

"I have two cats, Beemer and Romana, and I keep a Golden Retriever, Paco, for a friend of mine.

"Paco has epilepsy and the seizures usually last about ten minutes. He is so scared before he has one and he always tries to let us know when a seizure is coming. His whole body stiffens and all he can do is lie there until the seizure runs its course. A veterinarian had recommended that he be put on phenobarbital. His owner had refused and one day I had the opportunity to use The Radiance Technique® during a seizure. He had nudged me and then began to lay on the floor as his legs stiffened.

"I quickly drew the Cosmic Symbols and I put one hand on Head Position #3 (although my hand covered most of the top of his head) and my other hand on Back Position #2. As the seizure progressed, I moved my hand from Back Position #2 to the base of his spine. The seizure duration was a little over 5 minutes. I massaged him after the seizure ended and he slept for about 15 minutes. Once he had rested, he was lively and very active. Since then, he has been very insistent about nudging my hands to put on his Heart Center. (During the seizure when I first put my hands on Paco, my inner voice directed me to move my left hand from his Heart to the base of his spine.) He is a wonderful being and I am honored that I can assist him with the process of his seizures.

"My male cat Beemer enjoys hands-on. After I had studied The First Degree, he would stretch out on the bed in the morning for a brief hands-on session–his purr would deepen and intensify. He still goes through the ritual of the morning hands-on before we have to get up.

"Romana, my female with *personality*, loves The Second Degree. She, too, had enjoyed The First Degree but The Second Degree was enjoyed even more. It has now gotten to the point when she hops on my lap for her evening cuddle, she will take her paw and grab my free hand to put on any point on her body (usually her Heart Center or her head). She usually doesn't like anybody to hold her–except me. I'll pick her up and she'll settle in my arms and purr while I pet her.

"I live next to State game land and in the Fall, I have deer in my yard. One time, I parked my car and saw three of them. I drew the symbols and they stood still while we watched each other. They were so beautiful and seemed to understand that I meant no harm. There was such a stillness while our minds and hearts connected.

"I also did The Second Degree on all my shrubs when I cut them back for their Winter rest. I also did Shantis with them to thank and honor them for their growth and to help them with their dormant state. It took me the greater part of a morning preparing them. I'll probably do the same thing in Spring. "

Lyn Gilbert
The Second Degree
Pennsylvania

The use of hands-on is a genuine discovery process for you. These sharings encourage you to go beyond what your mind knows about yourself and just move with love. Animals move naturally toward radiant energy and grow from their contact with us, and we grow from our radiant interaction with them. The response to radiant energy which is loving and harmless can be surprising and profound as in this sharing about an encounter with a snake:

"Recently I had the unusual opportunity to share radiant energy with a snake. Rainbow, a five-foot-long boa constrictor, was the object of much attention at a friend's birthday party. Everyone greatly enjoyed her presence, and she warmed to all the attention by wrapping herself around whoever was close by.

"At one point, Rainbow decided to favor me with her company, and coiled around my waist. I responded by applying radiant energy, my left hand right under her neck, my right hand over her midsection. Rainbow immediately became very calm, resting her head gently upon my knee. There she stayed, while I alternated hand positions down the length of her body. The other guests had no idea what was going on and were fascinated by Rainbow's tranquil reaction to me. 'Look, he's hypnotized the snake!' someone exclaimed.

"The hands-on continued for a half hour, after which Rainbow expressed her gratitude by affectionately nuzzling behind my ear. Then, she quietly crawled away. This experience proved to me that everything, including 'emotionless' reptiles, responds to the healing power of love and radiant energy we are so blessed to share. I'll never forget this encounter."

Van Ault
The Fourth Degree
California

Many families share TRT with their own or friend's animals as a part of everyday activity and as special needs occur. This sharing from Canada involves several different animals:

"Our 11-year-old long-haired tabby cat, Willow, has suffered a great deal from neglect by her former owner. Two front teeth have fallen out. She has been quite sick from pneumonia, and has had a big problem with dermatitis due to a flea allergy. A pill once a week would help control it, but that created other problems in side effects. Since I have learned The Radiance Technique, I have put my hands on her back near her tail, the worst area for the dermatitis. She has not had a pill in many weeks and the veterinarian says that her back is in pretty good shape, although somewhat tender, and he has never seen her fur so fluffy. Six years ago I groomed her by taking scissors and simply cutting out all the tangles, they were so knotted. Every time I sit down, Willow is there, wanting up and wanting me to touch her. She would be there for hours, purring, if I let her.

"My 15-year-old son works at a store that sells exotic pets—fish and reptiles. A rather rare baby Baja, California, king snake was left under a light too long and my son found him with his mouth open, looking rather dead. My son was able to revive him but the snake was rather sluggish. Three or four times a week, I would hold the Baja snake in my hands for awhile. It became more active and when I would approach the container to pick him up, he would have his head up towards me. He seemed to know it was me. Unfortunately, he was stolen from his container just when I had decided I would buy him because I had become attached to him while giving him hands-on. I do direct energy to him, hoping he is all right.

"Several other snakes were stolen at the same time as well as a White's Tree frog being boarded for a customer. I have been directing energy for all the missing creatures and the tree frog came back before its owner returned from holiday. None of the others have been recovered, however.

"Maggie is a wild-caught ball python purchased by my son. She (or he) refused to eat, no matter what was offered. After almost six months of Maggie refusing food, my son asked a friend who has studied to The Third Degree (3A) of

11

TRT to do some energy balancing with Maggie to help her to eat. Before the session, Maggie did pass some waste material. Since she hadn't eaten, this waste was from food caught in the wild more than six months before. While our friend was holding Maggie and doing the energy balancing with the Attunement Process, Maggie stopped moving and remained perfectly still, her head and neck suspended in mid-air. As soon as our friend finished, Maggie would start moving again. This happened three times in a row so it was not a coincidence. Maggie felt something different.

"Ten days later, Maggie ate and has eaten regularly since. She was very fussy at first, eating only beige rats. She is now one of the most beautiful ball pythons, very firm and round and very contented. According to our friend, Maggie had been mistreated by the people who caught her and she was very afraid and didn't trust anyone. All that has changed."

Linda Whitlock
The Second Degree
Canada

Here is another sharing from someone who was visiting others and experienced a surprising response to radiant hands:

"I was visiting a friend's backyard with a group of students. The beautiful Florida weather was being soaked up by all of us, including my friend's cat which, I later found out, was not very friendly to strangers. Curiosity got the best of her, however, and before long I felt her soft fur rub against my leg as I was stretched out on a towel.

"My friend said that the cat might stay if I did NOT touch her. Instead, the cat kept pushing against me and meowed as if she wanted me to pat her. With one hand I rubbed her tummy, while the other caressed her head and back.

"She reacted as if she were being hypnotized, rolling over and going completely limp all over. She remained this way for 30 minutes or more. Thereafter, whenever I was around, she followed me and jumped into my lap as soon as I was sitting down."

Nancy Hopkins
The Second Degree
Florida

Animals can also be attuned so that they, too, may expand from within their use of universal energy. Many use their feet as hands to groom themselves and to touch other animals and their caretaker. "Paws-on" is a common phrase in many radiant households where the animals have been attuned to The First Degree or beyond.

When I travel, I am usually fortunate to have another person with The Radiance Technique who will care for my cats. However, a few years ago, when my cat who had been attuned to The First Degree and beyond needed a caretaker, I used a friend's service who had not studied the technique. She never fully understood what was happening but remarked over and over about how the cat had placed herself on the caretaker's back "just exactly where it hurt" and how it felt better every time she slept on her this way.

In Chapter 7 we look more deeply into the service that animals give to us. We know from our own experience that having animals attuned is a support for them and their growth as well as a support for ourselves. It is a joyous, harmless, wholing and healing benefit for every living being.

An Authorized Instructor shares her first experience with attuning a cat:

> "A cat named Whisky had a dramatic change of personality after he was neutered at the vet's. He went from a very playful, mischievous and affectionate kitten of eight months to a cat that was morose, solitary and disinterested in the world and people around him. He began wandering out at night–every night–and coming home the next day marked from brawls and hiding from the people he lived with. He was only affectionate at mealtime and as soon as dinner was over, he was off on his solitary, nocturnal prowls. He was definitely not the cute little kitten his caretakers had fallen in love with.

> "I decided to attune him to The First Degree of TRT. He (usually) was not keen to be picked up . . . and would bite or scratch. However, I scooped him up on my lap, with my hands on his heart and shoulder. I immediately began The First Degree Attunement Process. And I continued with the hands-on and used the technique for directing of The Second Degree, directing the radiant energy to all body positions.

"I was there for nearly two hours! There was no doubt Whisky was soaking up the energy and was definitely in 'cat heaven' for those two hours.

"I am glad to report that The Second Degree cat Whisky has become a little more like his affectionate and loving self, and is more open to being picked up and given love. He also stays home most nights now, although he is still given to nocturnal wanderings.

"This is the first animal I have attuned to The Second Degree and is an honor for me."

Chaysten Besso
The Third Degree (3B)
Australia

Most Authorized Instructors will explore with you the possibility of attuning your animals to The First Degree or The Second Degree for their growth and development. There is also an addresses section where you may write for more specific contacts.

THE SECOND DEGREE: USING HANDS-ON AND THE COSMIC SYMBOLS

If you have taken The Second Degree, you have an expanded capacity for hands-on. Often close animal friends notice this difference in your energy field when it happens. They are naturally open to you and your energy all the time without analyzing the difference they may sense.

In your class, you also have learned how to use the Cosmic Symbols as you are using hands-on with yourself and others. Remember to add the Cosmic Symbols to your hands-on process with animals as well. They are very responsive to the Cosmic Symbols. Create Cosmic Symbols as you pet and touch the animal, or pattern them into their energy field as they rest or cuddle with you. Each time you use the Cosmic Symbols to access radiant energy, you are on a deeper discovery journey and sharing this discovery with your animal friend is a deep form of communication and bonding.

DIRECTING ENERGY

Alumni of The Second Degree and The Radiant Third Degree learn ways to direct energy and to deepen their inner interactions with the one they are sharing energy with. Everyone who has studied The Second Degree and beyond can use these methods for adding to their radiant energy outreach.

If you've taken The Second Degree or beyond, explore imaging the Cosmic Symbols moving through certain parts of the animal's body that may need support and healing. This allows you to interact within the inner planes when radiant touch is not possible such as when an animal is hospitalized or at a distance from you for whatever the reasons.

Following is a sharing where hands-on and directing energy as well as networking were combined to help a family's dog:

> "When our family's older shepherd Bambi had a violent seizure, she began shaking so much that I was barely able to hold her. I couldn't even let her go enough to do my Cosmic Symbols on the physical plane. My husband, Art, also has studied The Second Degree and he began networking immediately in the Los Angeles area. Within a few minutes of the networking telephone calls, Bambi stopped shaking and we were able to do hands-on. We are very grateful for everyone's participation. The seizure has not recurred and Bambi has been in good health."

> Mary Lyndall Scott
> The Third Degree (3A)
> California

DIRECTING, USING COSMIC SYMBOLS AND HANDS-ON

Even when you travel, with The Radiance Technique,® you are never absent from your loved ones. Communication and contact are immediate as you direct energy to them from wherever you are, through the inner dimensions, no matter where they are geographically located. The following sharing combines directing energy, using Cosmic Symbols, and hands-on with TRT to support an injured kitten:

> "My three-month-old kitten fell from the first story stair landing to the basement floor–a drop of approximately 12 feet.

> "Because I saw her fall, I began directing the universal energy while she was falling. I immediately ran down the stairs expecting to find her heaped on the floor. She was not there. I moved into the basement looking for her and

drew Cosmic Symbols with my hands. I soon found her huddled under a piece of furniture. She appeared stunned, wide-eyed and totally still. Her position under the furniture allowed me to place one hand on the side of her body. She felt cold and like a rock. She was not bleeding and appeared to not have any broken bones. She seemed to be hardly breathing and was so still.

"I placed my other hand on my heart to support myself and transform the fear and guilt I was experiencing. Almost immediately I was aware of being in a time-less space and there seemed to be no separation between the two of us. I seemed that we were there for hours. Afterwards, I checked my watch and realized that by 'clock' time it probably was about seven minutes.

"She carefully moved from under the couch and took a look around, flipped her tail and bounced up the stairs. She currently can be seen dangling from ledges, tree limbs, fence gates, etc. She has no fear about falling.

"I watched her carefully for several hours after this event to make sure that there was no internal injury that would require a visit to the vet. No visit was necessary and many thanks for this cosmic first aid kit. (You can't leave home without it.)"

Lily Sowell
The Fourth Degree
Oregon

In the techniques learned at The Second Degree and beyond of TRT you are present and at one with the animal beyond the outer planes definitions of time, space or distance. Through the use of the Cosmic Symbols you are accessing universal energy and strengthening the inner connection that you have with all that is alive. Should you choose, you may also direct radiant support to endangered species and animals that you may not be near who need your support for their very existence.

When you direct energy, set aside the time to go through the whole process and spend a quiet and meditative time with the animal or animals. You may gain deeper insights into the crisis or healing process of the animals as you direct energy. You may also learn a great deal about the nature of the animal itself, deepening your bond and loving relationship.

Expand your interactions beyond the animals that you know well. Collect photographs from magazines and newspapers to support your projects of interacting with endangered species. Various issues of *The Radiance Technique Journal* include sharings from those who have been working with this project for some time. Use the photographs to assist you as you image the animal that is endangered. Then continue with the process for directing energy as you were taught in your seminar for The Second Degree. (See Chapter 7.)

ATTUNING WITH ANIMALS

Many alumni join the High Noon Peace Network using their capacities for directing energy and/or attuning. The following sharing involves the sharing of human and animal during this special energy bonding time:

"As I sit now on the sofa, my lap is being warmed by the very peaceful body of my spoiled terrier mix, Bucky. He has been resting there now for 1 ½ hours, during my High Noon and directing of energy session.

"Bucky doesn't usually spend much time on my lap unless I'm giving or receiving attunements or radiant energy, or have just done so. At breakfast, for example, Bucky usually likes to sit beside my girlfriend's foot, while she tickles his tummy with her toe. But, if I've already done my first attunements of the day, Bucky insists on my lap instead!

"(Bucky wriggles now as my focus has shifted to this writing—and my sketching him on my lap—but a few Cosmic spirals quickly settle him down again.)

"It is lucky that none of our friends object to the little fellow lying on them as they receive their hands-on sessions because Bucky just won't stay down.

"Fortunately, our larger dog, Bindi, has better manners—as she is a 30-kilogram Labrador-ridgeback mix! However, she does try to snuggle some part of her body into our laps when possible."

Kay Hardy
The Third Degree (3A)
Australia

For alumni who have completed The Third Degree for Personal Growth, Enhanced Radiance and Transformation (3A) and beyond, you can use the Attunement Process to include animals—those who live with you and those whom you wish to support. As your Authorized Instructor suggested, animals are much more mobile than humans and do not always "sit still" for the Attunement Process. Use the inner planes Attunement Process for them when they are nearby or in your lap. Also carry photographs or clippings from magazines for using the Attunement Process with different members of the animal kingdom. Set aside a time each day to direct your Attunement Process to animals. You might chose the High Noon time period in order to join the inner planes Peace Network or you might find a regular time in the morning or evening.

Following is a sharing from a student who uses the local newspaper to help with her support of the animal kingdom:

"Every week my local paper publishes a picture and description of an animal 'up for adoption.' I cut the column and use TRT to direct radiant energy support for the animal in finding an appropriate and loving home.

"I also place the animal's picture onto my heart center with my universal heart-hands and I have had some profound discoveries about universal love and its dynamic presence in *all* living forms."

Lily Sowell
The Fourth Degree
Oregon

Magazine or other photographs become valuable resources to have with you to support the time that you have set aside for interacting with animals. Newer plastic globes of the earth now feature animals as part of the printing on the globe, locating the countries or areas where the animal may be found. These, too, are wonderful tools to support your Attunements with endangered species. (See Chapter 4 for more information on interconnecting with different animals.)

Love is the Key.
Barbara Ray, Ph.D.

The following is reprinted with permission from The 'Reiki' Factor in The Radiance Technique,® *by Dr. Barbara Ray,* © *1992. It is Chapter 12 in that book.*

CHAPTER TWO

PETS, PLANTS AND THE RADIANCE TECHNIQUE®

All living things—both plant and animal—are linked in an extraordinarily designed, ecological balance. Man has an essential role to play in this chain of regeneration.

R. Buckminster Fuller

The Radiance Technique accesses vital, universal energy and therefore can be used effectively on anything that is *alive!* Animals and plants are an integral part of our planetary system, and their destiny is linked with ours. Certain species of animals and plants are becoming extinct because mankind in modern societies has forgotten his *connection* with other living creatures. In our journey toward wholeness, we will all have to learn to share this planet with the native animals and plants who not only have the right to be here but also are a vital, integral part of our entire ecological system. Animals and plants exhibit an awareness different from ours, yet they share with us intelligence, natural growth cycles, health, disease, and death. Different does not mean inferior!

In the area of health and disease, animals and plants are affected as are human beings by the ravages of polluted air, water, and food sources. Because of their close contact with humans, domesticated pets share to an event greater degree the maladies currently arising in contemporary life. In recent times, pets have increasingly incurred diseases similar to ours. Motorized vehicles are constant sources of accidents and death for our pets. Pet psychologist have appeared on the scene to help when pets display emotional disorders from close contact with distressed human beings.

Recently, *Time* magazine did an article on the use of massage therapy for pets suffering from physical stress caused by the pressures and rigors of modern life. *New Age* magazine featured a story on chiropractic techniques for animal. Of all the books available on wholistic health and natural healing, few offer a separate chapter on animals and pets. This book does. The Radiance Technique can be used with your pets and plants harmlessly. Let me share a few of the many experiences I have on record of using TRT to help pets, nondomesticated animals, and plants.

A user of TRT in Atlanta received a call from a local veterinarian to assist him with his own dog. His four-year-old female Great Dane had jumped a barbed wire fence, missed, and mutilated the entire undersection of her body. He had operated on his dog twice in an attempt to get the skin and wounds to heal but to no avail. He was attempting one more operation to remove the massive amounts of dead skin. At this point, a student of TRT from the Center in Atlanta began giving the dog daily sessions before and after the surgery in a series of five hands-on sessions averaging thirty to fort-five minutes each. Within this small amount of time, the Great Dane healed beautifully. The veterinarian was grateful for discovering TRT and believed its universal energy saved his dog's life.

A five-year-old male Schnauzer named Erich, belonging to a friend of mine, suddenly contracted the devastating parvo disease. His owner had been gone all day and had returned home late in the evening. She noticed the dog was listless and not hungry. A couple of hours later, she discovered large amounts of dried blood that he had vomited. Realizing that hew was severely ill, she took his temperature and found it was nearly 106 degrees. He was extremely dehydrated from diarrhea, and his body was ice cold. She rushed him to the veterinarian at 11:30 p.m. In the car, a friend gave Erich hands-on of TRT all the way to the office, and his icy skin became lukewarm. The doctor gave the dog an appropriate injection but told my friend that it was doubtful the dog would survive the night.

After returning home, she called several people who were trained in The Second Degree of TRT, which includes a highly efficient method for distance directing of radiant energy. They agreed to help by sending Erich healing energy. By the next morning the dog had improved but still was not "out of the woods." Another friend, trained in TRT, volunteered to go to the clinic and to administer complete hands-on sessions on Erich. The veterinarian was open to any help offered. In just two days, the dog had almost totally recovered and, to the amazement of all, including his doctor, Erich was eating normally and regaining energy and strength. To verify the disease, a blood test was taken. The test showed a positive reading—it was parvo. The dog had made a remarkable recovery in an unheard-of short time from a perilous, frequently fatal disease.

Erich's TRT hands-on sessions continued on a daily basis, sometimes twice a day, to restore his energy level and eliminate all the effects of the devastating disease. Use of this technique literally had saved his life. It is important to note that the dog had been receiving hands-on sessions from its owner for nearly three years before this episode. During these years, she had found TRT to be an extremely effective preventive technique for all her pets, including two cats. Her vet bills were low, and her pets were maintaining high levels of positive health. When parvo hit her dog, his preexisting positive health level and life-energy reservoir from the TRT sessions diminished the overall impact.

Now for the dramatic story of Buckwheat, who has become known as the "miracle dog of Atlanta," as told by his owner in edited form. Late one evening in June, eight-year-old Buckwheat sat on the patio watching over his backyard domain. He had shared a late-night piece of cake with his owners. Suddenly, two large dogs jumped the fence and attacked the friendly, easygoing hound dog. In the ensuing battle, his neck was nearly broken, his ears torn, his throat bitten, and he suffered severe liver damage. When his owners found him, he was in shock, dazed, disoriented, and near death. The veterinarian did all that he could but Buckwheat did not respond well. He was losing vitality daily.

In July, a friend who had studied TRT came to see him. Lynn knew immediately that he needed more help than the medication and nursing care were providing. She gave the hands-on session of TRT to Buckwheat for an hour.

Days went by, and Buckwheat continued to get worse. His muscles were degenerating, the saliva glands were not functioning, and his weight dropped from thirty to fifteen pounds. The veterinarian concluded that his liver was damaged beyond repair and, regretfully, recommended that the dog be put to sleep. Lynn was informed of the situation and thereupon began

21

a series of intensive hands-on sessions on Buckwheat. In addition, when she went home at night, she used the distance directing method of TRT Second Degree with him. Lynn felt that, through TRT, she was able to feel intuitively the dog's vital energy level as well as his will to live.

With all the sessions he was receiving, his energy level increased, he regained use of his neck, ate well, and actually barked–the healing process had begun. It was "uphill" from that moment on. Now that he could finally eat, his diet was enriched with whole grains, fresh vegetables, meat, and eggs and always more of TRT! Several weeks later the vet examined him again and could not believe it was the same dog–even Buckwheat's liver *appeared to have regenerated itself*: the vet actually thought he was another hound dog. But the scars and torn ears, though healed now, validated Buckwheat's miraculous recovery.

I have not yet had the honor of meeting Buckwheat, but his gracious owner studied advanced levels of TRT for Buckwheat, for herself and for her husband! She told the class of Buckwheat's "special radiance tale" and assured us that "his upset emotions and trauma had disappeared and that he had completely recovered his sense of humor, his playfulness, charm, and friendliness." With ongoing use of TRT, Buckwheat had been restored to health, to wholeness and to life.

Many people who have taken TRT seminars have reported how effective its use has been in treating a wide variety of disorders of dogs and other pets. One many found TRT helpful in getting his German Shepherd through her epileptic attacks. One woman's sixteen-year-old poodle had been suffering from severe coughing attacks and excessive liquids in the lungs. She used TRT each day on her dog and, within a week, these symptoms had reduced significantly. One woman reported that she used the hands-on on her dog's head every day for only ten minutes, and his highly tense, volatile energy changed to normal. In one class, one woman called TRT a "pet lifesaver" in stopping bleeding. Hit by a car and badly bleeding from a leg wound, her dog lay dying in the street. She ran out and used TRT, which immediately stopped the bleeding. With the help of friends, she got him to the vet, who expressed amazement at what had happened. He affirmed that without the use of TRT, the dog would have bled to death before she could get him to help.

It has been my experience as well as that of many others that cats respond well to the universal energy of TRT. They seem to be able to "tune in" naturally and with ease to this life energy. I am a fond lover of cats. For twenty years I have always had at least two cats, sometimes as many as five, as regular members of my household. In addition, several others are always passing through. For years I have consistently given my cats the hands-on of TRT. I have found that overall they are healthier, brighter, and less frequently sick. My vet bills are lower. When the cats have needed medical treatment, it has tended to be less costly, the recovery has been quicker, and the side effects have been lessened.

I had an interesting experience with a stray who took up residence at my front door until I admitted her into the family and named her Buffy. As it turned out Buffy had cancer of the bladder in its advanced stage. But, the TRT hands-on sessions used with her helped her relax and seemed to help the pain. The side effects of the medications were so potent that after consulting with the vet, I finally took her off the high doses and relied solely on the use of TRT. Buffy was a very lovely cat but a very sick one. Yet, with TRT, she was able to eat and maintain her weight. When additional internal complications arose, she made her transition. She had, however, given me the opportunity of sharing her inner light and of learning how to treat sick animals with TRT.

In Atlanta, I have done a considerable amount of healing work with cats. As a result, the Center there frequently got calls for help with cats. One of the diseases we often encountered was feline leukemia. It is a devastating disease that strikes a cat suddenly, draining it of its vital energy and almost certainly resulting in death. Because it is a highly contagious disease, the ill cat is treated in its home. Special precautions are taken with cleaning my skin and clothes to avoid spreading it to other cats as well as to my own when I return home.

Several years ago, I received a call from a dejected, extremely upset, and deeply saddened owner of a wonderful three-year-old Siamese cat named Sylvia. Misidentified as to gender early in kittenhood, Sylvia actually was a boy! He had severe feline leukemia and had been sent home by the vet with the gloomy prognosis that death could be expected shortly. His despondent owner had decided to seek additional help.

When I began doing TRT hands-on sessions with Sylvia, he was completely lacking in vital energy. He was near death and could barely eat, and his eyes were glazed over–he was in the dying process. I gave Sylvia TRT sessions nearly every day for the first few weeks. On the third day, he was perched in the window at my "usual" arrival time. With TRT, the connection between us had been easily opened. Thereafter, his owner reported that he always knew when I was coming and would sit in the window for my car.

When I began using TRT with Sylvia, there were places on his body where his fur had fallen off, and he had large bluish-colored sores on his head, neck, and shoulders. During the early part of this process, his condition appeared to get much worse. He could barely move, he was extremely dehydrated, the sores got bigger and bluer, and he lost more fur and much weight. In the natural healing process, diseases sometimes get worse before reversing. TRT promotes this *natural* process but often reverses the disease sooner and then moves in the direction of restoring health.

His owner was distraught at how horrible Sylvia looked. She kept checking with the vet, who reassured her that Sylvia could not be harmed and reminded her that his illness was terminal. I had added Sylvia's name to my distance healing list. As is my custom, I direct healing energies to everyone on the list, people and pets, each evening. I also asked Sylvia's owner to play a certain record for him several times each day using a wholistic approach to healing even with pets! With TRT as the primary direct source of Light-energy, I sometimes use secondary sources—especially certain musical pieces.

The process we went through with Sylvia taught me many things that later opened dimensions of understanding in my healing work with others. On evening while I was directing healing using The Second Degree, I had the experience of becoming *one* with Sylvia. It was as though I was inside him. I could see and *feel* the disease. I could clearly see the Light-energy accessed by TRT inside that cat, and I could see it as fire burning the disease *out* of him. That insight helped explain the horrible blue sores and all the draining pus. Outwardly, Sylvia was a terrible mess of sores, pus, skin, and bones. Inwardly, he was being transformed. I could also see that the negative was being *transmuted* into positive energy—it was pure White Light.

It was an incredible process to behold. I was deeply grateful for the opportunity to go through this experience with Sylvia. Since then, many people who have studied TRT have shared similar experiences with me. With TRT, you direct this Radiant, Light-energy and become a co-worker in the healing process. With TRT, you are *not* using your personal energy nor are you in any way controlling the outcome.

I worked with Sylvia for more than two months, sometimes daily, sometimes with distance healing only. About midway in this process, he appeared to be ready to die at any moment. Then suddenly, he accepted food, a light returned to his eyes, and gradually, he began to regain strength and vital energy. He needed all of this radiant energy he could get! At that time, I was not an instructor of TRT and therefore could not teach this technique to Sylvia's owner. But, I knew deep inside of my being that I would one day become one so that I could teach those close to a pet or loved one, family or friend, how to use this profound and harmless technique.

Meanwhile, Sylvia's vitality was restored completely. The laboratory reports indicated that the leukemia was no longer present. His new fur was thick, shiny, and beautiful. One day in early fall, I stopped by to give him another hands-on session. I knew when I saw this healthy, playful very much *alive* Siamese cat that he would not need any more hands-on from me. In his own special way, Sylvia let me know that day that he was completely well. Usually, when I began his hands-on session, he would settle down and quietly let me proceed. That day, however, with twinkling eyes, he playfully chewed my fingers, rolled around, and brought me his toys to play "fetch." With loving energy, Sylvia let me know his healing process was completed! It was my last visit with him, but occasionally through the months his grateful owner called me to let me know that Sylvia was fine!

People from all parts of the country have shared with me their experiences with TRT and cats. After receiving only the first of the TRT attunements of The First Degree, one woman reported to the class that she had gone home and used TRT with her cat, who had been listless and not eating. Within minutes, while she was administering TRT, her cat threw up a strange-looking substance, then ate her dinner, drank some water, and returned to normal. I instructed her to continue using TRT with he cat for several days to balance her energy and restore *ki* to a normal level. She did, with positive results.

One man reported that his six-year-old cat had suffered a broken leg in an unusual fall. The leg, though set properly by the vet, was not healing as it should have. I recommended that he give the cat thirty minutes of the hands-on of TRT each day, which he did. Within five days, the improvement was so enormous that the cat was going outside dragging its cast and leg. Previously, he had stayed in a corner, listless and depressed.

A woman in Minnesota said that she had taken in a stray cat who had been severely mistreated and then deserted by her owners. The cat had suffered severe emotional damage. She was afraid of people but had become aggressive rather than passive in her behavior. She would attack and bite people—even guests who came into her new owner's home. The hostile behavior continued for several years. Then her owner studied TRT, both The First and Second Degrees. She then used it with her cat on a regular basis for several months. When at work during the day, she was able to direct radiance at a distance to her cat. Within four months, the improvement in the cat's personality was noticed by all who knew her. She began relating to people without incurring scratches and bites. TRT had touched the non-physical level of her cat-being that had been bruised and battered. Her owner has kept me updated on her cat's continued progress. She reports that the cat "seems to enjoy life more now. She is less tense and now hardly ever exhibits her old, 'spooky,' jumpy, scared self." With use of TRT, her healing is in progress, and she is gaining wholeness in her cat-life experience.

Sometimes in our lives, each of us might have the opportunity to help animals other than our pets. In each of the cases I am about to describe the opportunity came to me unexpectedly. I was thankful to have the gift of TRT and to learn more about the animal kingdom that exists around us all.

I had attended a soccer game in Tampa, Florida, and had been impressed by the vigor of the Rowdies, by the incredible spirit of the crowd, and by the joyful array of colors filling the stadium. Upon leaving the game, we were sitting in the midst of a traffic jam when off to my right I saw something move in the grass near the curb. Since traffic was stopped, I got out and carefully approached what turned out to be a seagull, no doubt one of Jonathan Livingston's relatives, with a badly broken wing. It appeared that the bird had been hit by a car and abandoned. Having had no previous experience with injured, undomesticated animals, I stood there for a moment wondering what to do. The seagull could not be left there. He could not fly, he could no longer fend for himself, and he would not survive. Remembering how effective I had found TRT to be in calming people, I took a deep breath, stepped forward, and reached out for the seagull with radiance in my hands. He fluttered and stumbled a few feet. I stopped–he stopped. I proceeded toward him again, picked him up, and got into the car. Immediately, I could feel this radiant energy pouring from my hands into his entire body. I have always loved seagulls but had never touched one and never held one in my hands. I could hardly believe this was happening. It was an incredible experience. Without TRT, I know that I would not have had the confidence to touch that seagull.

With the hands-on of TRT, he calmed down and absorbed the vital energy being shared with him. The seagull seemed somehow to know what this universal energy was–he seemed to know instinctively that it was harmless, healing, life-force energy. He seemed to absorb it with his whole being. I was vividly aware that the energy flowing through that seagull was the same energy flowing through me. The contact was there. He never once tried to bite me even though I did not have his beak covered. We drove from Tampa straight to the Suncoast Seabird Sanctuary in Indian Rocks Beach on the Gulf, north of St. Petersburg, Florida.

It was after midnight, dark, and cold but, after we had rung the bell several times, a sleepy but kind, gentle, elderly man admitted the seagull for treatment. I went to visit him the next morning. He was doing remarkable well after surgery. He had lost a wing, but he could still live a useful seagull-life, taking care of himself and doing his part in the ecological system. I had learned a new dimension of using this profound technique and, through it, had learned a great deal about the expression of the life-force energy of this planet.

About a year later, while I was walking along the seashore, I came upon a cormorant twisting around dizzily in the sand. I called to a friend for help. Using the TRT hands-on, we managed to get the bird calmed. We used a towel over his long, active beak to avoid bites. Holding the cormorant in my lap, I began using TRT with this beautiful aquatic creature of nature. We went straight to the Suncoast Seabird Sanctuary, where it was determined that the cormorant had been a victim of poisoning, probably from polluted water or food. This cormorant could, however, be saved with antibiotics. We both continued doing TRT distance directing of radiant energy on this bird until it was released from the sanctuary.

Not long ago, I came across another lovely cormorant on the beach who was also in trouble. Somehow the bird's left leg had been so badly broken that it could not fly or move very far. Realizing that the bird was too alert for me to handle without proper equipment, two of us trained in TRT began directing this energy to it. We could only get within a couple of feet of him. Once again, I drove to the Suncoast Seabird Sanctuary for help. Earlier that day, staff from that sanctuary had tried to catch this cormorant but the bird had gotten into the water and avoided the net. With the TRT Light-energy in contact with the bird, I knew he was ready to be helped.

Through TRT a direct connection of healing, radiant energy had been provided, letting him know that it was safe to accept help. He was calmer and more trusting now. This time, a friend and I used TRT without touch the bird physically, and he was captured and treated. His leg healed and soon he was set free. TRT was an essential tool for use in helping this beautiful but severely injured bird. Without such an effective technique, I might have been just another person passing by the bird, sympathetic to its plight but not knowing what to do.

Modern scientific research has given us much information about plant sensitivity and plant awareness. Caring for household and garden plants is rewarding though serious endeavor. We have evidence that plants respond to our love and caring attention and that they shrink from attacks by people and pets. Accessing universal, Light-energy, TRT is a highly effective tool for use in working with plants.

One woman shared her exciting experience with growing a summer vegetable garden and using TRT. She reported, "I held each seed in my hands pouring radiance into them. I seemed to be able to sense the life-force energy within the seeds in connection with the use of TRT coming from my hands. When the seeds began sprouting, I would carefully cup my hands around the small plants for several minutes. In the process of using TRT with my vegetables several times a week, I myself experienced a deep sense of inner peace. I felt as though I had been one with the natural growth cycle. I was much less tense and more centered than I had ever been in my life. I was also doing the hands-on session with myself early each morning. The beautiful, full, large vegetables my family and I ate all summer were the reward of my efforts. My friends and family were amazed at my gardening success that summer in contrast to my previous failures. There is simply no doubt in my mind that using TRT was the ingredient responsible for such abundance."

Now for the famous rubber plant story of Atlanta. During the second session of a seminar, a woman brought in a pathetic, nearly dead rubber plant. She had gotten it for twenty-eight cents at a local K-Mart. With barely a spark of life in it, the little plant was green-brown and sagging in its pot. In the previous class, I had discussed the use of TRT with all living things, including plants. But I will have to admit that when I saw her bringing in that more than half-dead plant, I myself had a moment of hesitation. I took a deep breath, continued the seminar, and directed radiant energy to the plant for all I was worth!

Others in the class helped by using the hands-on of TRT from its roots up, which is the best place to begin. The vital, radiant energy can then be carried upward and distributed. Several months later I had occasion to talk with this woman and, tentatively, I asked her about the plant. With enthusiasm, she responded that it had grown incredibly! She had taken it to her office and often put it under her desk to direct this radiant energy to it between her feet all day. Everyone in the office had watched in amazement as it got bigger and bigger. Pieces had been cut, and additional offspring of this gigantic plant had been given away. The story of this once nearly dead rubber plant with its "healing" through TRT became "widely" known! There is no doubt that with TRT this plant had progressed in its natural evolution to wholeness and, in the process, its story had touched all of us deeply.

Many people have reported similar experiences with TRT and their plants. One man wrote of his success in growing roses using TRT; another told of the healing and re-energizing of his favorite willow tree. A woman in Florida shared her experience of using TRT distance directing of energy with her delicate flower bushes and citrus trees during the hard freeze in 1980. By spring, her yard was in full array, lush with budding life. Her neighbors, who had lost their plants, were amazed at the abundance of her yard. Hers was the only living, green back-yard on the block!

The purpose of this chapter has been to share some experiences about how effective TRT has been with pets, other animals, and plants. There are many additional ways TRT could be used in this context. One of the unique aspects of TRT is that it provides a connection for vital, Light-energy, which can be used creatively, efficiently and harmlessly, and adapted to any situation by the person with the "touch of radiance."

CHAPTER THREE

DAILY LIFE–
DYNAMIC INTERACTIONS WITH ANIMALS

Sharings from people who have used TRT with their animals help to make this a real guide for adventures with animals of all kinds. Each person has a way of coming to grips with daily life with animals and although there is the common thread of using radiant energy, the situations that are shared include the full spectrum of life–crises and quiet moments–sadness and laughter. Sometimes life is intense for the human or the animal and, luckily, each day can also bring simple moments of real joy and bonding between animal and human. The depth and breadth of these shared events help demonstrate the use of The Radiance Technique® with animals and are here for all of us to grow from. They offer joyous suggestions that can be adapted to any family or individual.

In this chapter we are including a full spectrum of ways to use radiant energy through your use of hands-on, directing of energy, use of Cosmic Symbols and the Attunement Process. Whatever degree you have studied, you can use the sustaining and universal energy of The Radiance Technique® to assist you and your animal friends in your life every single day.

Children are especially varied in their use and responses. They share radiant energy because it feels good to them and to their animal friend. A teenage student of The First Degree writes:

"I have just recently taken The First Degree of The Radiance Technique® and I am fourteen years of age. I think The Radiance Technique® is a wonderful thing. I have a hamster that was miserable, but over the past

30

week I have done 10 minutes a night of hands-on with him, and now he's cuddly and friendly. Also my cat, Pookie, got attacked by a dog last year. She had a severe hernia and wounds on her back. My mom did radiant hands-on with her and she recovered wonderfully. I'm glad I have The First Degree."

Kirstin Wood
The First Degree
Canada

Families find a different unity with one another as they help with the animals in their household and those outside and nearby. In the following, a mother shares a portion of her family life with her teenage sons who have also learned The Radiance Technique and tells about their hands-on use with animals:

"My twin sons built a leafy shelter for an entire family of hedgehogs and spend hours of the summer watching and tending their needs. A baby hedgehog named Ball developed a cold and was given hours of Radiant hands-on. Indeed, so was all the family, sometimes for hurt noses and tiny feet, sometimes for the delight of the twins of holding them. Never were any spikes put out by the hedgehogs. Many have been the birds, hedgehogs and baby frogs brought in from the park for varying ministrations, some needing veterinary care, and all tended with Radiant hands.

"Leo, who was given to us as a kitten, was initially quite uptight, bolting away on sight from anyone other than ourselves. Gone in a flash! And pursued by the twins who would then lie on the floor holding him with Radiant hands. Recently, he sprinted into the room and started dancing and rolling around going up to everyone in turn."

Anne Keltie
The Fifth Degree
England

What a joyous variety of uses these teens and young people have found for sharing radiant energy. The possibilities are truly endless. Whatever happens in daily life with animals can be supported with radiant energy, harmlessly and unconditionally.

In the daily lives of all of us, situations occur that call for extra support, and this is true of animals as well. They join us in our stress-filled lives, they have accidents. They may have the need for surgery or medical attention. Just as you have a daily hands-on time for yourself, it is important to also have a "hands-on" process with your pet or animal friend. When you begin early on in your relationship, the animal becomes eager for this bonding and sharing time. Sometimes, as we have suggested "hands-on" may actually be done a few inches above the level of contact with the skin or fur of the animal, while the animal is sleeping or resting. This ongoing daily support contributes to the overall wellbeing and health and prepares the way for times of extra need.

CREATING THE LIGHT-HABIT OF HANDS-ON

The following sharings express what happens when you have the light habit of hands-on:

"When I attended The Third Degree (3A) seminar, I was told we would learn the attunements with animals so that I could do attunements on my cat. After the first day of the seminar, I just went home and innocently gave it a shot and my Siamese didn't *need* to be 'held'– she just blissed out and turned to butter!

"Now, however, she's more than accepting hands-on sessions–she's demanding them! *Every night now*–at 8:00 (you can almost set your watch by this behavior), I have a cat on my lap worming her way under my hands. If I don't happen to be sitting down at the time, she'll come and find me and scream at me until she gets her hands-on!

"People who have come over for dinner and don't know about her 'program' are amazed. At first they think she just wants to sit in my lap, but after a few minutes she's lying on her back, eyes closed, legs just dangling in mid-air, hardly breathing and obviously in a state of complete relaxation. It's a position that can't be missed–especially when it goes on for 5 or 10 minutes at a stretch!"

Linda Hedquist
The Third Degree (3A)
Iowa

"I use the hands-on with animals quite often–not always intentionally I might add as they do tend to appear whenever it's happening. I have been working with my cat Jessie's skin allergies for months. She is typically a mess during the flea season, which is lengthy down here.

"I have been able to cut down her dosage of cortisone with continued application of radiant energy and am expecting to do away with the cortisone all together one day."

Ann Healy
The Third Degree (3A)
Alabama

Another student shares a similar point, that his cat seems to "know" clearly when he is using TRT to access radiant, loving energy and the cat appears on the scene:

"My big, black tomcat, Lucis, can always tell when radiant energy is moving in our house. I never have to go find him, because even when he's snoozing soundly in one of his little hideaways, he becomes alert to the energy shift, and seeks me out. Anytime I do attunements or direct energy, he comes to me, demanding to participate in the process. Naturally, that means getting on my lap, and soaking up as much radiance as he possibly can, while purring contentedly. Lucis has been my correspondence "model" for directing energy to all kinds of people, places, events and situation, and truly a partner in healing. He was given The First and The Second Degree by an instructor several years ago. The name Lucis means light and this handsome, radiant kitty truly lives up to his name."

The same student goes on to share a unique underwater experience:

"I wondered if The Radiance Technique works underwater. It was a question I had answered while snorkeling off the coral reef near Key West, Florida. I was the only human in the water at the time, and as I swam across the reef, I began patterning the Cosmic Symbols I had learned at The Second Degree in the sea. It was awkward at first, but I slowly continued patterning, swishing the water around with my hands. I could see no sea creatures anywhere around as I began, and just as I thought I'd stop patterning, a huge school of small, silver colored fish rose from somewhere beneath me. I continued patterning, and the fish, as if mesmerized, barely moved, hovering in the water a few feet beneath me as I floated on the surface, looking down at them.

"This went on for some minutes, until I had to return to my boat. It was a quiet, very peaceful energy exchange, as we interacted in a field of radiant energy that seemed to permeate the water. This experience reminded me that TRT is an *inner planes* science, first and foremost, and physical conditions are not an impediment to its capability."

Van Ault
The Fourth Degree
California

RADIANCE IN THE SEA

Another student reports the joys of radiant interaction in the sea:

"When I was vacationing in Hawaii, I had the opportunity to go snorkeling and feed the fish. I was told that they like frozen green peas best, so, well armed with round green ammunition, I set out to conquer some fishy hearts. Well, for a moment or two, anyway.

"On the way to the dive site, I did hands-on with the peas and used the Cosmic Symbols I learned at The Second Degree.

"Once in the water, I began directing energy and was quickly surrounded by finny friends eager for a handout. I soon ran out of peas, but the fish kept coming. I was wearing a mantle of 60 or 70 fish, all pushing and shoving to touch me. I was still using the symbols and now it seemed I was expected to do 'hands-on.' I did. By holding my hands out in front of me, the fish were able to swim under them without feeling 'caught.' They swam around and rubbed my hands like cats being petted. They ranged in size from about an inch long to a foot and a half. All colors. All shapes. All beautiful.

"Through the cloud of fish I saw another shape approaching, and it was BIG. The warning about sharks in the area flashed through my mind, but before I could head for shore, I realized it was a scuba diver. My new friends scattered, giving my hands one more brush or my face plate one last nudge. He signaled me to surface, and when I did he asked what I'd been feeding the fish. It seems they were coming from all over the reef for whatever bait I was using. They even left people who were feeding them green peas. I told him I was giving them green peas and radiant energy."

"My hands tingled all the way back to my hotel, and even now, if I close my eyes, I can feel the soft bump of a silver-scaled nose asking for some Light."

Helen Woods
The Second Degree
Arizona

Following is a sharing from a student of The First Degree who has used the support of hands-on with TRT with different animals:

"I received The First Degree in 1985 in a group composed mostly of people involved with animals. I would say that The First Degree has helped me hesitate before calling the vet. To wit:

"I received a call about a month ago from a neighbor who had two frightened young men in her house. They had just hit or run over a dog–probably a golden retriever–mine. I ascertained that the dog was not in serious shock, had no compound fractures or obvious fractures. She had been hit in the hip area and was in too much pain for me to take her temperature.

"Casting about in my mind for a vet I could raise Saturday evening, I started doing hands-on with her. At some point the shaking stopped. Later she dragged herself to water. I elected to postpone subjecting her to X-rays, and kept postponing it over the next few days, using hands-on with her whenever possible. Within a couple of weeks she became completely sound–the whole family cheered when the battered tail began to wag again.

"I have an 8-month-old colt who has developed a lump on the shoulder. Again, I dreaded to call the vet as I know it would be a matter for surgery. Whenever possible, I have been using hands-on with the foal; it's not as simple as with the dog since the foal is a 'handful. Anyway, the lump has ceased growing, and I believe it is getting a little smaller. Time will tell.

"Although I've never been terribly convinced of the effectiveness of modern medicine, in our framework it

35

has been the only option available. The Radiance Technique® provides another option."

Betty Sue Carroll
The First Degree
New York

A Surprising Litter

A student in Canada shares how an unusual litter was supported by the use of hands-on with the mother:

"Our smallish dog, Pee Ginny, began receiving loving radiant energy as soon as her pregnancy was noticed. This went on for several weeks and then the dog had a miscarriage of seven tiny fetal pups.

"The vet said that the pregnancy was over. Dogs don't have partial miscarriages, he said.

"But our dog's belly continued to swell and I continued with daily highly appreciated energy sessions. Soon, five robust puppies were delivered. The vet declared that our dog would never have survived giving birth to a litter of 12. Mother and pups are all thriving."

Lana Douglas
The Second Degree
Canada

Another student shares the importance of hands-on when an animal has just been through surgery for spaying:

"I have been intending to write you for a long time about my experience of using The Radiance Technique® on my grandson's dog. Cindy is a female dog, about one year at the time of being spayed. I knew from the experience of my own former dog, who had the operation at the young age of 6 months, that they suffer a lot the first day or so, or even longer. My husband and I had suffered with our dog, because she was so pitiful in her pain.

"So when I heard my grandson's dog was to have the operation, I went to their house to be there to help it with The Radiance Technique.® I held the dog on my lap, and applied my hands directly to the incision area. Of course, she could not climb to my lap, or jump up on my lap as usual. I also used hands-on for a short time on her head. That was on a Thursday evening. By Sunday she was jumping about as usual as if she had not had surgery 3 days earlier.

"This was considerable improvement over the actions of my own dog who was six months younger, and took a week to return to normal activities. The Radiance Technique® apparently cut the recuperative period in half and lessened the pain considerably. If I had been there to use hands-on with her daily, it would have been faster. Total time of hands-on application was about 30 to 45 minutes. Needless to say, Cindy loves me as a true friend. Any time I go to their house, she is quick to greet me, and get my hands on her."

Mrs. Clytes Cullar
The Second Degree
Texas

In my own experience with a female kitten named Lotus Love, who had been spayed and immediately pulled out her stitches, the hands-on was a vital part of supporting her through the "strangeness" of having surgery and stitches. Her brother Sunshine was neutered at the same time and they both came home from the animal hospital together. The vet and I had discussed keeping them together this way so that neither kitten would be "strange" to the other smelling differently from one another on return. Male neutering usually doesn't require stitches. Indeed, Sunshine was more playful and more active his first day home. However, she was quiet and very annoyed by her stitches and her shaved belly.

Lotus Love licked and licked this odd skin without fur and pulled at her stitches. When she succeeded in getting them out while my back was turned, I called the vet to see what to do next. Luckily, the real closure for the incision was made with internal stitches that dissolve naturally. The vet explained to me how to use an anti-infective (hydrogen peroxide) to clean her abdomen (there was almost no bleeding), and to watch her to see if she had any other difficulties. She reminded me: "She got rid of what was unnatural to her so she'll probably be fine now."

And, indeed she was. She responded by allowing me more time with hands-on, although I was careful to keep my hands above the level of contact when I was near the incision itself until the next day, and even then, I used a very light touch. She was "herself" again, playful and full of lively interactions in only three or four days and really responded to the hands-on time we had with one another. Of these two kittens, brother and sister from the same litter, she is more inclined to do "paws-on" with me, cuddling nearby and placing her head and paws on my shoulder and Heart Center. Both love receiving the radiant touch of hands-on.

DIRECTING ENERGY WHILE THE ANIMAL IS AT THE VET'S

Students who have studied The Second Degree and beyond remind us constantly that one of the most practical uses of TRT is directing to an animal that must remain at the vet's and cannot during that time receive the hands-on contact. When my kittens experienced their overnight stay at the vet's during their neutering, I directed energy and attunements to them and requested my network of friends to join in. Following is a sharing that describes a joyful misunderstanding that occurred while directing energy with an animal at the vet's:

"In response to your request for experiences with The Radiance Technique® with animals, my mother and I would like to offer the following.

"My mother's supervisor has an elderly Shitzu named Gertie. Late one afternoon Gertie stepped on a bee, was stung, and went into shock. Her owner rushed her to the vet who began emergency treatment (including putting the dog under an oxygen tent). He did not expect Gertie to survive more than a few hours, and told the owner so.

"When my mother went to work that evening and heard about what had happened, she phoned me and asked me to begin directing energy using The Second Degree with Gertie. As soon as she had a break, she also began directing energy. From about 6 p.m. to 3 a.m., Gertie was receiving continuously radiant energy.

"At 3 a.m. I woke up and, as I normally do if I have fallen asleep while directing with someone, began to re-initiate the directing of energy. About halfway through the first symbol, however, I had a very strong feeling of 'don't bother–it's not needed anymore.' 'Poor Gertie,' I thought. 'Guess she didn't make it.' At the same time, my mother felt what she described as a release of tension–'like a spring snapping back' was her description. She was certain that Gertie had died. Also at 3 a.m., the owner, who had been unable to sleep for worrying, thought, 'It's all over now. Poor Gertie–I'm sure going to miss her,' and finally succeeded in going to sleep.

"At 3 a.m., 'Poor Gertie' sat up under the oxygen tent and barked. The vet is still shaking his head and saying, 'It's a miracle. That dog was dying.'"

Elaine Fuller
The Second Degree
California

An in-home accident provided this kitten with ample need for hands-on:

"Ananda, our young Siamese kitten, was injured when a large potted plant fell onto her tail. The veterinarian reported her tail had a compound fracture and that judging from the X-rays, the nerves had been completely severed. He set the tail as best as he could but said that at most Ananda would have a limp, paralyzed tail with no feeling.

"We took Ananda home and worked with the hands-on of TRT directly on the tail for about five hours. Ananda was still groggy from the anesthesia and slept the whole time.

"Over the next two weeks, we continued working with hands-on sessions every evening and weekends 30 to 60 minutes each day. We, of course, combined these with directing energy and radiant attunements.

"We are now in the fifth week (at the time of writing) after the accident and her tail stands fully erect and has feeling and movement down to the tip. Ananda has been very receptive to the hands-on sessions."

Jim Lightenheart
Erick Larson
The Fifth Degree
California

An accident with a car provided an opportunity for this dog to have a network of friends providing radiant energy for her support:

"About six months ago, our German Shepherd was hit by a pick-up truck. Lassie could not walk. The news from the vet was not good: She needed surgery. Since there are seven people in my family with The Radiance Technique, we began our work. She received long periods of hands-on, much directing of energy from those who knew The Second Degree, and many, many attunements.

"One month to the day of the accident, she stood up, licking our faces and hands. Her wholing process continued and today she is healthy, well, walking and, yes, running.

"Unbelievable, the vet said. Best of all, the quality of her life has not been impaired. What a wonderful, joyous tool we have."

Blanche Hanks
The Fourth Degree
Oklahoma

CONNECTING WITH COSMIC SYMBOLS

Several alumni have shared the importance of using TRT and especially the Cosmic Symbols learned as part of The Second Degree seminar to help them call "lost" animals to them. This sharing describes how The Second Degree use of TRT makes an inner connection, a universal bond that occurs even with animals that you don't "know" very well:

"I was visiting my friend in Alabama. A few days before the incident I'm about to describe, we found a stray cat begging for a home at the Waysider Restaurant. We brought the cat back to my friend's apartment.

"A few days later, she took the cat to the vet for shots and to be examined. Upon leaving the office, the cat 'freaked out' and jumped out of her arms, apparently traumatized by the visit to the vet. She ran off into the woods between the vet clinic and the adjacent building. My friend called her but she did not respond. My friend was upset because she had to leave to see a client at her office. On her way to the office, she stopped by the apartment to tell me what happened. We were both very concerned as the temperature was expected to drop considerably that night.

"I told her I would go look for the cat and not to worry. I've had excellent success in the past in drawing upset animals (my cat, Ziggy) out of the woods using The Second Degree technique. So, I went over to the place she described immediately and attempted to draw the cat out of the woods. I immediately set up the Cosmic Symbols over the following scene: I imaged the stray cat walking toward me and allowing me to pick her up and put her in the car. Usually I pair this with calling the cat's name, but in this case I didn't know her name so I called, 'Here, Kitty, Kitty.' As soon as I did this, a cat came running toward me out of the woods–but it was the wrong cat! It was Emmett, the vet's cat!

"So, remembering to be persistent, I tried again. Within a minute or two I heard a rustling and then the stray cat allowed me to see her. We made eye contact and she approached me, but as soon as I moved toward her, she ran off. This happened twice. By this time, it was beginning to get dark and I knew time was running out. So, I altered the 'scene'–I set up the symbols again and used the same image but imposed a time limit. I said I wanted her to come to me *within five minutes*. Within two minutes she was walking toward me–this time allowing me to pick her up and take her to the car.

"Within the five minute time period, she was in the car and we were driving home!!! I was truly amazed! I felt that was the 'acid test' because this cat didn't know me very well or have the relationship with me that my own cat had (we've been together 12½ years!). I didn't even know her name and she responded to the radiant energy!

"A few days later I had the opportunity to use this technique again with Ziggy who had run into the woods prior to the car ride back to Augusta. Not only did Ziggy come to me, but so did Cagney (one of my friend's cats), a neighborhood cat, and a nearby dog! I felt like St. Francis of Assisi–drawing all these animals toward me at once.

"I was interested to read that someone tried a similar process with whales, with similar effects! That was very exciting to me and reinforces my own experimentation. It is essential that we continue to share our results and network with each other!"

Faith Stayer
The Third Degree (3A)
Georgia

FOLLOWING RADIANT ENERGY HOME

Sometimes the networking help of many people supports the universal inner connection and helps the 'lost' animal to follow the radiant, Light-energy of TRT home as in the following:

"DendurLion, one of my two cats just vanished one Sunday afternoon a few weeks ago. She has a pattern of staying out for a stretch of four to five hours, but come 10 p.m. Sunday night, I knew something was amiss. I went out calling for her, and immediately began patterning the Cosmic Symbols I learned in The Second and Third Degrees of The Radiance Technique.® I also did extended hands-on with The Second Degree technique and began using the Attunement Process I learned in The Third Degree (3A). I got the sense she was all right physically—that she just couldn't get home. Maybe someone had taken her in. She's pretty special; I wouldn't blame them!

"The next morning, I continued patterning, weaving her a path home with the Cosmic Symbols, a string of light to follow home. I also phoned several friends asking for support and networking for DendurLion's well-being, her finding her way home, and also support for my other kitty, Loretti, who was experiencing separation trauma. Everyone I contacted was extremely supportive and cooperative, sharing ways to use the expanded hands-on to guide Dendur home. In addition to their own support work, they passed on the information to other alumni of The Radiance Technique® with whom they spoke throughout the day, and on Monday night, there was a coast-to-coast (and beyond) light networking for Dendur!

"For five long days I went out calling. I put up posters. Through it all, the shining difference was The Radiance Technique® and its various applications for Dendur, for Loretti and me! I knew—it was a knowingness beyond a sensing or a feeling—deep in my heart that she was safe, and being supported beyond any means my mind could imagine.

"Then on Friday afternoon, I heard this 'whoosh' like a tiny and very intense burst of wind and there she was! Dusty, like she'd been in a basement or toolshed, hungry and very pleased to be home. She would scamper from me (she was really hungry) to be petted and held (five days without a radiant touch) to the food and water bowls, and walk by Loretti to get sniffed . . . and eventually cleaned.

"I want to express my heartfelt gratitude for this incredible art and science called The Radiance Technique® and to all those who supported us through this

42

experience. The support and light networking of so many was an expansion beyond words–and one I highly recommend. You don't have to wait 'until a kitty runs away!"

Shannon Orrock
The Fourth Degree
California

For the two different cats in this sharing, neither of whom were lost, the Cosmic Symbols made an inner contact to bring them out of hiding for their caretaker:

"We have been having a bitter cold snap this past month. When my husband and I went to bed one evening, we weren't sure if Tasha (one of our cats) was in or out. Since it was down to the lower teens already, I was worried about her being outside. I kept waking periodically, going to the door to see if she wanted in. Finally, instead of fretting over it, I decided to do the Cosmic Symbols to connect with her (using The Second Degree) and direct energy to her. I had barely started, still awake, when I heard her talking. She jumped into bed with us. I concluded The Second Degree connection is when she became aware of how worried I was about her. (It amazes me how they can find hiding places–I had looked 'everywhere' I thought!)

"Our other cat, Pumpkin, adores to have Cosmic Symbols rubbed on his head, manipulating his head and your hand till you do it.

"Just thought of another incident. Tasha was limping badly. We decided to take her to the vet, made appointment, etc., and then could not find her. When I started walking around the outside of the house, connecting mentally with The Second Degree, she came out of her hiding place under a bush. Her foot was swollen with some infection, so the vet drained it and she recovered nicely."

Kathy Gruba
The Second Degree
Nebraska

The dilemma of animals experiencing travel by air is a very real concern. In the following a student shares how she used the directing of energy and attunements to help her and her cat:

"After we got settled in Germany, my husband and I went to the States for a short holiday and to pick up our

43

cat, Schatje, from my parents-in-law. On our return journey we flew out of JFK Airport, New York. This was the first time that Schatje had flown and she was naturally terrified. We stayed with her in the terminal building for as long as possible before turning her over to the airport staff, who would take her to the animal section of the plane.

"Once we had boarded the plane and were preparing for take-off, I started to direct Attunements to Schatje. I connected with her and could feel her heart beating very rapidly. I continued to direct Attunements to her throughout the take-off and then I 'built' a circle of Attunements around her, so that every time she moved in her transporter, she would move into a circle of comforting energy.

"Shortly after the roar of the engines subsided to a constant hum, I felt her heart rate slow down to a normal speed. Throughout the rest of the 8-hour journey, I checked with her every so often, by directing an Attunement, to see how she was coping. With each Attunement that I directed I was able to feel her heart beat and assess her level of anxiety.

"After she arrived at her new home in Stuttgart, she quickly inspected her surroundings and then tucked into a big meal almost as though nothing had happened."

Linda Gareh-Applegate
The Fourth Degree
Germany

SHARING ATTUNEMENTS

Sharing the Attunements for The First and/or The Second Degree has continued to be a growth experience for Authorized Instructors who have had this unique opportunity. The following sharing demonstrates how deeply we can become involved with the animal and ourselves in relationship with animals:

"This sharing is about the transformation of a noble horse and what happened with my 'present from the universe.' A girlfriend of mine in a nearby city phoned me one day in despair to ask me what to do about her Arabian thoroughbred stallion. She complained that 'Tiamat' (this means 'the old earth') had become so wild and dangerous that she was the only one who dared to care for him. She could not go for the holidays for one day because nobody else dared to clear the dung. Besides, Tiamat was skinny and did not like her to break him in.

"I offered to share The First Degree Attunement Process of TRT with the stallion. After a short time, Tiamat went through a transformation. Encouraged by this improvement, I also shared The Second Degree Attunement Process with him. In only half a year, Tiamat had become the friendliest horse you can imagine. He even let my then two-year-old son ride on him. I also tried it and enjoyed it very much. Tiamat reacted to every little order. My boyfriend, who did not know how to ride a horse at all, wanted to go at full gallop. Tiamat just did not speed. He is a horse that attunes to the rider's abilities. He has become beautiful, gentle and easy to handle, while still keeping his vivacity.

"My friend was so grateful and enthusiastic about the effects of what I had done that she wanted to give me beautiful Ganja, Tiamat's younger sister, as a present. I asked for time for reflection. First, I was thrilled. A horse of my own, and such a beautiful Arabian one. A dream of my childhood seemed to become true, and I ordered a trailer coupling for my new car, already envisioning myself travelling to my different seminar locations accompanied by Ganja. I felt loved by the cosmos.

"Just to be sure, I directed energy to this project. The feedback was very clear and unequivocal: 'That's not a good idea at all. You are a single, busy mother already. A horse is not a car you can put into a garage. It needs as much care, love and attention as a child. You would have to neglect your work, your son or the horse, or probably all of them, suffering from non-stop stress. Where you live, there are riding possibilities just around the corner. Be satisfied with this.' I was shocked and realized at the same time, that 'the universe' was totally true. I relaxed, cancelled the order for the $500 trailer coupling and embraced the situation. Perhaps, in a few years, my little son who is now four, gets into horse-riding, too, and we can have a horse of our own then.

"I am grateful for the powerful tool I have with TRT to come more and more into the natural flow of my life and get to know what really supports me on my way."

Barbara Simonsohn
The Fourth Degree
Germany

45

The very real inner bonding that happens through using TRT with animals supports your own growth process in many different ways. Another student writes about this deepening of inner contact with The Radiance Technique:

"Exchanging love with the whales trapped off Point Barrow, Alaska, gifted me with an even deeper awareness of how addictive patterns restrict experiencing the fullness of Life. Acceptance and Radiant Persistence are gateways to unlimited Freedom ... a Celebration of Knowing."

Katie Reich
The Fourth Degree
Alabama

DON'T FORGET TO PLAY

Along with supporting animals in a crisis or deepening our bond with them, using TRT helps us as humans to expand our sense of play. With her permission, we'd like to share from the entry "play" from Dr. Barbara Ray's book, *The Expanded Reference Manual:*

"Play is a form of acting and recreating. Regardless of age, all humans need some time and activities of playing. Play is a part of your wholeness and ongoing sense of well-being in whatever cycle you are processing. TRT accessing Universal Radiance gives support to your need to play–to express laughter and tears, to perceive yourself in many creative ways, to relax and to learn ever-expanding knowingness of Life's many and endless varieties of expressions, to grow naturally and to transform."

Animals are great guides for lively times of play since they do it naturally, and all the time. You most likely enjoy playing with a dog who retrieves a ball or chases a stick or a cat that plays with a string. When you don't appreciate their "play" time, you're often looking at consequences rather than joining in the play itself. If you live with cats, you might experience their "midnight madness" frolicking as aimed at keeping you up, taking their actions personally instead of enjoying their all out "go for it" energy.

As you watch a friendly kitten leap into a sink half-full of water or fling the books out of the bookcase as it bounds in and

46

out . . . or you see a puppy entangle in the curtains as it tries to retrieve the ball or thump its tail so vigorously that things on a nearby table topple to the floor, put your hands on your Heart Center and laugh. After all, they don't know the consequences might be a mess, they're just playing!

Love is all there is.

Barbara Ray, Ph.D.

A kitten is so flexible
that she is almost double;
the hind parts are equivalent
to another kitten with
which the forepart plays.
She does not discover that
her tail belongs to her until
you tread on it.

Henry David Thoreau

CHAPTER FOUR

THE UNIVERSALITY OF ALL ANIMALS: HELPING AND LOVING ANIMALS OF ALL KINDS

Within the kingdom of animals are an infinite variety of creatures, from mammals to fishes and from reptiles to birds. Each has its own way of being, its own needs for survival and its own place in the world of living energies that humankind has divided into categories. These categories have been devised to keep track of similarities and differences. They also help us to study relationships–those of animals to human, of humans to animals and of both to the environment.

Many resources are helping us all to make the connections about the relationships that various animals have to the survival of the environment–our mutual environment–the Earth. In this study of environment and relationships, it is vitally important to see the relationship that humankind has to animals.

AN EMPOWERING WAY TO MEET ANIMALS IN YOUR HEART

An exercise that everyone who has studied The Radiance Technique can do, from The First Degree onward, involves the use of your radiant, heart hands and your willingness to spend a few minutes of your day in meditation with the different kingdoms that make our Planet Earth the interdependent realm that it is. In *The Expanded Reference Manual of The Radiance Technique,*® Dr. Barbara Ray writes about this powerful "interconnection" on page 57:

"In higher consciousness, interconnection refers to the 'inner-connection' from *within*, from the Inner Seed of Life and Light of all living things. All life is inner-connected from *within* at the same *vibrational* point of Light. In using TRT, you have a gateway–an opportunity to grasp deeply the inner-connectedness of all Life."

Reprinted with permission
Copyright © 1987 Barbara Ray

In many workshops Dr. Ray has invited students to create a time for meditating and directing the harmless and loving energy of TRT to the planet. You might want to schedule your Discovery Exercise during the High Noon Networking for Peace. As she has written in *The Expanded Reference Manual* on page 84, the Peace Network is for all alumni to "join together worldwide each day at High Noon in your own time zones to apply radiant, transcendental, universal energy with yourself while focusing your attention on the planetary outreach of peace. . . . Share your experiences in your awareness journal as you touch into the radiant inner planes network interconnecting all of us with one another and all living forms from *within*." It is a wonderful way to be in touch with all of the life forms on the planet. We are giving you the following Discovery Exercise which has been adapted from ones that Dr. Ray has shared and which other students have shared in *The Radiance Technique Journal.*

EXPANSION–A DISCOVERY EXERCISE WITH YOUR HEART CENTER

You may want to have a globe, or a picture of the planet nearby as you begin you networking time. Begin by placing your radiant hands on your Heart Center. If you have studied the use of Cosmic Symbols, also create them in your Heart Center, or if you know the Attunement Process, use the Attunement within your own Heart Center to expand and support yourself and your meditation.

First, image a spiraling rainbow bridge of light reaching from your Heart Center outward toward the planet. Then, with a conscious invitation, bring into your heart representatives of the mineral kingdom. Let your image be whatever comes at the moment. You may invite grains of sand from the great deserts of the world or stones from the rivers; you may welcome the crystals or "precious" gems that form naturally or the deep lava that encrusts the volcanoes. Whatever appears in your image, bring it through the spiraling rainbow bridge of light into your heart. Spend a few minutes bringing these varied parts of the mineral kingdom into your heart. Notice what rests in your heart. Become very aware of all that you see there. Feel and enhance the support with your hands in your Heart Center. Then, gently send back to where they came from, each of these representatives of the mineral kingdom sharing your loving support as they spiral in light back to their homes.

Next, invite the members of the plant kingdom to come into your Heart Center. Allow time for whatever appears to rest in your heart. You may welcome trees or flowers, or shrubs and meadow grasses to come into your heart. Again, just let whatever appears to you come into your heart. Each time you do this radiant meditation, it will be different. Spend a few minutes becoming aware of the plant kingdom, honoring its powerful support of your life. Then, gently send the representatives of the plant kingdom through the spiraling rainbow bridge of light back to their natural habitat, seeding them with light and love to expand their journey.

Next, invite members of the animal kingdom to spiral through the rainbow bridge into your Heart Center. You may find dogs and cats or giant elephants or tiny birds and fishes accepting your invitation to rest in radiant energy in your heart. Allow the meditation of these wonderful companions on the planet to continue noticing which animals come into your heart and supporting them with your loving hands. Notice each one or each group of animals and share your loving energy with them, seeding them with the Light-energy of TRT. Then, gently return the animals to their natural surroundings through the spiraling rainbow of light.

Now invite into your heart members of the human race through the spiraling rainbow bridge. You may be surprised to see faces or nationalities that you do not know very well or you may have close friends or family members resting in the radiance of your hands and your Heart Center. Continue to meditate with these human companions on the planet as they move into your heart. Notice everything that you can about them. Honor them and support them with the loving and peaceful energy that you are accessing with The Radiance Technique. Then, gently invite them to return to where they came from, carrying with them the light and loving support that rests in your heart and your hands. Take all the time you need to rest in this Light-energy that you have created and notice your own Heart Center and how you feel.

After a few minutes, allow yourself to become aware of the room around you and the things that are near. Take the time to make some notations in your own journal of your experience. Each time you experience this Discovery Exercise it will be different. You may want to share it with others or to write to *The Radiance Technique Journal* so that the editors may share your experiences with others. There is a special section on animals and on networking for Peace in each issue. (See addresses on page 116.)

One student who used this Heart Center meditation shared his responses to the invitation to have members of the animal kingdom enter his heart:

"For me, immediately the great elephant sauntered in through the spiral, and also eagles–both ones I remembered seeing in a zoo once as well as eagles I had seen flying free–and dogs; many friendly dogs spiraled in.

"(When we) remembered the plant kingdom, the flowers and forests of all continents, and the wheat, the corn, the green life force on the planet. These we spiraled into our hearts and then seeded them back out onto our planet, the Brazilian rain forest, the Black Forest, Kansas wheat, meadow flowers.

"We invited the mineral kingdom into our hearts through the spiral, and for me the mountain ranges, the Rocky Mountains, the Himalayas, the Urals, the Alps, the Catalinas and waterfalls like Niagara Falls, Angel Falls, Vernal Falls, Yosemite Falls all cascaded into my heart through the spiral.

"And, yes, we invited humanity into our hearts through the spiral, and we remembered the peoples of all continents–the Chinese, the Eskimos, the Americans, the Australians, the Asians and Europeans, the Mediterranean, the Africans. They spiraled into our hearts in light and then we seeded all back from our hearts onto our planet with a spiral bridge of light."

Michael Young
The Fourth Degree
Illinois

51

LEARNING TO LIVE IN HARMONY WITH ANIMALS

One of the most important distinctions to make in looking at living with animals either in your home or nearby if you have a farm, ranch or just a few acres in the countryside is to notice who has the major responsibility. It is clear that humans have a very different consciousness than animals do. Humans know they exist. Animals do not have this important awareness. This is an incredibly different way of seeing the world.

Animals are dependent on their instincts and their location for their survival. They have no consciousness of their existence. They forage for food—they do not "fix" or grow their food. When we take them in to live with us, we take over this very simple yet very important responsibility. In addition, we promise in that moment to maintain their health, their environment, to care for them—in other words, to become conscious of them as living energy systems. Animals cannot and do not accept this kind of responsibility.

Yet, in the ecological balance of our world, they play an equally important role in our health and well being. And, animals in the wild—all kinds whether mammals or insects—help achieve the natural balance necessary for a food chain that results in food for humans as well. They contribute to the forests, the grasses, the lives of other animals. All are part of our natural world which actually includes everything from weather patterns to food production. Subtle and not so subtle changes occur when these more natural patterns of existence are disturbed by humankind in the building of cities or the creation of recreational areas in the "wilder" parts of the environment. These man-made changes affect every living system in the environment.

Many alumni are concerned about planet Earth and all its living inhabitants. One shared his feelings about the different expressions of life on our planet and how to interact with the acceleration of extinction of certain species:

SUPPORTING LIFE ON THE PLANET

"Our universe began, we now believe, some 15-billion years ago. According to a PBS television special, 'The Creation of the Universe,' 'Everything that there is or can be was contained . . . within a single spark of energy rapidly expanding, but still smaller than the nucleus of an atom and ruled by a single primordial law.'

"We call that primordial law a blueprint that contains in living essence all we can think, know or be. As Dr. Barbara Ray has written in *The Expanded Reference Manual* in the entry for 'inner planes– . . . All planes derive from the Inner Source of transcendental Light–inner-connected with the Universal Creative Principle. The outer planes are manifested form coming from the inner plane blueprint.' (Reprinted with permission © 1987, Page 56.)

"Life, consciousness, oak trees, snails, you and I were there in essence as the universe began–the living essence of all things in our universe we call Universal Principles.

"The first glimmers of life forms–our planet earth's biosphere–appeared almost 4-billion years ago. In the millions of years that followed, species appeared and stabilized, manifesting the transcendent, inner-living blueprint.

"The ancient Egyptians revered each species as the expression of a vital Cosmic function. The practice was a meditation used to support and clarify an essential function of the Universe *within oneself*, to know the whole Source by honoring its expression.

"The expressions of life on our planet are not only a direct connection to this living blueprint of the Universe, but also all species are repositories of millions of years of hard-won lessons of adaptation and survival.

"In the process of growth of the earth's bio-sphere–which is itself a living being with the oceans as the earth's blood system and the air its respiratory sys-tem–there have always been extinctions and evolvement of new species.

"However, it is estimated that during the next three decades an average of 100 species a day will become extinct. This is a rate of 1,000 times faster than has ever prevailed since pre-history. And with the extinction of these hundreds of species the earth's entire eco-system declines, the very system that supports all life on the planet.

WHAT WE CAN DO

"As Dr. Ray writes in *The Expanded Reference Manual* in the entry for 'inner plane science', The Radiance Tech-nique® is 'an inner-plane science which 'accesses univer-sal, spirit energy from within you–the transcendental vibration inherent within this Radiance–within the Cosmos which creates all things.' (Page 56)

"It is possible for us through our connection with Universal energy to sew the damaged fabric of our planet's biosphere together. We can also support individuals and species through their death processes.

RADIANT EXERCISES

"With your radiant hands on your heart, image the essence of plants, insects, animals, etc. passing through your radiant hands and heart and seeding back into the Universe. You can also do this with the Cosmic Symbols, directing energy and with the Attunements.

"With the guidance of Dr. Ray, I have been doing this exercise for more than a year. Sometimes, I experience herds of animals galloping through my heart. The next day, spontaneously, may come insects or flowers–each day is different!

"Through this exercise I feel a living contact with the biosphere. Also, I am becoming more awake to my own capacities to function consciously on the inner planes of my being."

Stephen Love
The Fifth Degree
Germany

During what was called the (Persian) Gulf War in 1991, alumni of TRT contributed their help through massive networking efforts, directing of energy and attunements. A special interest in animals and the Earth itself led a Canadian student to share the following:

"I have been directing energy to the Earth and the animal kingdom in the Middle East:

"The cormorants drenched in oil, the fish, the whole Persian basin and marsh that are being affected.

"The flamingos that have been disturbed from their usual pattern of migration. How long will it be before they can return to their natural patterns?

"The camels wandering in the desert at night (and day) with all the shells and bullets whistling past and the planes overhead.

"And other types of birds. And the dogs and cats that don't get taken into the bomb shelters. Who talks to them to explain the confusion of what is happening? I know how my own dog shivers and shakes in thunderstorms or at the sound of kids' cap guns and air rifles.

"So, I direct energy to all the animals and birds.

"And, what about the assault on the Earth? Sea and land? The constant bombardment of bombs pounding and vibrating to Earth's core?

"What about the effects on the Earth and the animal, plant and mineral kingdoms? There is pain and suffering there, too.

"I've been dancing the Cosmic Symbols I have learned outside when I can (like tai-chi), directing to Nature, hoping for an understanding and a compassion for what the Earth's experience is in the Middle East."

Lorraine Wesley
The Third Degree (3B)
Canada

PROTECTION AND HEALING SUPPORT, OR EXTINCTION? A CHOICE FOR YOU!

Recognizing the universality of humans and the animals and plants as co-inhabitants of Earth helps us to take responsibility for our part in the overall task of creating a bountiful, abundant and healthy planetary environment.

In other chapters, we are looking more specifically at domestic animals, those that live closely with us in our homes or nearby outside. In this chapter, you will find empowering suggestions for using radiant energy with the non-domestic animals that you may meet–through motion pictures, in books, at the zoo, on television. There is a wealth of information about "wild" animals and their potential extinction. Many resources can help you to get in touch with how to help with hands-on, with directing energy and with attuning with animals in danger of becoming extinct. Following is a sharing of a discovery that happened near a zoo:

"While studying The Radiant Third Degree in London, I was drawn to walk along Regent's Canal, which goes past The London Zoo. Never having been there before, I was surprised and delighted to find that some of the animals can be seen from the footpath. I started directing energy to the various species and felt such joy and expansion as we 'danced together' in the universal energy. We talked later in the class of how we can connect with endangered species in the wild through their relatives in captivity."

Maya Fitzpatrick
The Third Degree (3A)
England

USING THE SECOND DEGREE FOR DIRECTING TO ENDANGERED SPECIES

You may want to begin your directing to endangered species by taking a photograph of the animal or your own visual memory of an animal in the zoo to represent other animals like it who are endangered. You can then direct energy using the photograph or image of the animal as the model for the actual living energy of the endangered animal. Often zoos are wonderful places to pick up postcard pictures of animals to carry with you for your directing energy projects. Many alumni keep a basket or notebook with these photographs handy at home for daily directing to endangered species. Choose a time of day each day, or set aside one day of the week for your service to the animal kingdom. Keep a note on your calendar or in your journal as a reminder so that you can make the light habit of directing energy an ongoing part of your life.

Then on the day that you have chosen, take the time to sit down and complete your directing with the animal or animals exactly as you were taught in The Second Degree or beyond, beginning with the use of the Cosmic Symbols to create your inner-connection, and then taking time to be with each *inner* hands-on position with the animal—four for the head, four for the front, and four for the back. Remaining in a meditation with each of the *inner* hands-on positions is a way to discover more from the inner dimensions about our animal companions on the planet. An appropriate time to remain in each *inner* hands-on position is not less than two minutes. Your choice to remain longer in each of these positions benefits you as well as the subject of your directing of energy. You can also use The Radiant Third Degree in this same way.

For those who have learned the Attunement Process through studying The Third Degree (3A), you can share the Attunement Process or a series of Attunements and then, continue to meditate with the animal following the Attunements, imaging the entire *inner* hands-on session. Many alumni choose High Noon to link with others supporting the Peace Network around the globe as their time to direct or attune with animals and the other life forms on Earth. This amplifies and expands the High Noon Peace Networking for everyone involved.

Another student discovered the one to one contact that is possible with animals while visiting a petting zoo far from home:

"When we think of Australia and its animal inhabitants, we primarily think about the two most publicized ones–the Koala bear and the kangaroo. Fortunately for the tourists who visit Sydney, Australia, there are several places you can encounter these beautiful animals.

"The one I selected seemed to allow for more hands-on petting, through it was an hour's drive from the city. Featherdale Wildlife Park offers a large individual petting zoo for the koala and for the kangaroo and its cousins, the wallaby, and the park has a large private collection of fauna indigenous to Australia.

"Many animals know a human by their scent and usually sniff you. When I entered the kangaroo and wallaby area, one wallaby approached me nose to nose!

"In this special moment, we exchanged our universal breaths–in a moment in eternity–of direct knowingness of our oneness of the life force regardless of our outer dressing. What a joy to just be–with the oneness of the breath.

"While visiting Australia, I became aware that radiant networking support is needed for the Australian Koala 'bear.' Experts in Australia report that more than 50 percent of all the Koalas living in the wild in Australia have diseases affecting both their eyesight and their reproductive organs. These diseases are curable with treatment.

"However, the Koala has a history of population decline. Originally, they were slaughtered for their skins, until they became a protected species in 1927. Over the past few decades, strenuous efforts have been made to insure the Koala's survival and they are now thriving colonies of them throughout eastern Australia.

"Alumni of TRT can join the network of those directing supportive energy to the Koala, for its continued survival and growth."

Yesnie Carrington
The Fifth Degree
Florida

Additionally, in almost every community there now exists a resource for helping animals that need sanctuary. This includes animals of all kinds. There are mammals such as the great apes that are in danger of extinction. There are dolphins and whales who are injured in nets and through hunting that may need protection and healing responses. There are reptiles such as the endangered turtles, and birds such as certain eagles and sparrows that are now being consciously protected by humans because their numbers are too few and they will soon be extinct unless such actions are taken.

In many communities there are Wildlife Rehabilitation or Animal Care and Control centers that help also to take care of local or regional creatures that are hurt or abandoned. The following is a sharing of a deep communication and expanding awareness:

"It was December 22 and the arctic freeze was upon us. My friend and I were walking in Golden Gate Park where we came across a domesticated white dove that had been abandoned. The dove was all puffed up from the cold and it did not look well. My friend said she would catch it and take it to Animal Care and Control. When she picked up the dove, she asked me to hold it and before I knew it a white dove was thrust into my radiant hands. It was funny to watch my mind saying, 'But, but . . .' and my radiant hands saying, 'Yes, yes . . .'

"Despite my gloves, my hands had been freezing all through our walk, even though we had walked quickly to try to stay warm. When I held the dove, my hands were suddenly vibrant and warm—I experienced a pulsating exchange between this little form and the radiant energy.

"I held the dove all the way to the Animal Care Center. Outwardly I was riding in a car to the animal center and inwardly I was learning so much in a silent exchange from this small white dove. I could *feel* the life force energy—there was no division of a greater or lesser being

58

and I was aware that I could make that kind of judgment—it was all the same unifying source.

"At one point, the dove drifted to sleep in my hands. I was attuning with it on the mental level as well. It felt as if there were no 'barriers' between us.

"I was aware that I did not know if the dove would live or die and at a deeper level (and to my surprise!), I wasn't upset or attached to an outcome. I was just so honored and filled with gratitude to have this opportunity to support another being no matter what happened next. I knew that this radiant support was a bridge, a 'cradle' into the next step whatever it might be.

"I was powerfully participating! (It was not my ego running around trying to 'control' things.) My radiant touch was accessing wholeness and radiant power and loving support. I have such gratitude to have TRT in my *Life* at any given moment, no matter where I am, no matter how cold it is outside!"

Leslie Christopher
The Fourth Degree
California

Sometimes the protecting organization grows from the needs in a community. Sometimes a particular individual or group helps the community come into an awareness by creating the service and publicizing it. One such needed organization is the California Marine Mammal Center in Sausilito, California. Following is a deeper look at their work and the experiences of using TRT with these large mammals:

"In ongoing celebration of the Purposes of The Radiance Technique Association International, Inc. (TRTAI), I want to share how Article #6 (See PURPOSES, page 114) deeply inner-connects with a very special part of my life—volunteering at the California Marine Mammal Center.

"The Center is an animal care facility for sick and injured lions and seals. It has as its purpose the 'rescue, rehabilitation and release' of these vital marine mammals. These animals are wild when rescued and great care is taken to support their wildness so that they can fully function upon their return.

"Over the months I have helped at the Center, I have become increasingly aware of how *natural* and *under-*

standing the energy of these 'wild' creatures is. I interact with the essence of the wildness–that 'just being'–through the use of The Radiance Technique,® a cosmic, natural science, and find my awareness of the Natural harmony of the essence of all life is expanding, expanding, expanding!

"In the continuum of rescue, rehabilitation and release, I use the precise system for accessing radiant energy through the use of hands-on application, the directing of energy through the Cosmic Symbols and the Attunement Process.

"When a rescue call comes into the Center, I inner-connect the radiant energy with the image of the animal before we arrive on the scene–to help ease any stress the animal may be in–and especially in the transition from the beach to the animal's new temporary 'home' at the Center.

"Once the animals are set up in their own large pens (complete with pool!), the volunteer crews are then responsible for their care/rehabilitation–from feeding to medicating to cleaning their pens. I will often 'clean' their pens with radiant energy, using the application of the Cosmic Symbols, as well as physically scrubbing them out.

"Feeding times are always a special joy as I toss fish into the pools. And since I help prepare their meals, my radiant 'heart hands' touch a lot of fish! That way I share my radiant touch even if I cannot directly touch the seals and sea lions (they can and do bite humans).

"For the sicker animals, we 'tub feed' them a fish mash formula. This tubing process can be quite a struggle for everyone involved, both humans and animals. If I am the person restraining the animal (holding him still), I gently place my hands on his head and direct energy with the Cosmic Symbols. I have experienced an energy of calmness moving through the animal for the duration of the feeding process.

"When breaks occur in our duties, I often walk around to the pens and inner-act with each seal or sea lion. It is in these moments of oneness with these beings that I experience a quiet peace–and such gratitude for this profound science.

"It is through these radiant communications that I can use The Second Degree technique of correspondence to inner-connect the animals to their species out in the ocean. I know I am supporting them *all* on the inner, even at this moment in time when their outer environment is increasingly becoming more polluted by oil spills, toxic chemicals, dumps, etc.

"Some animals die during their stay, while others recover and are released. Both types of 'releases' are profound—and I have experienced the vibration of an animal that just died, using that opportunity to support and nurture its being during transition.

"For those animals released into the Pacific, I will direct energy to them throughout the following months, supporting them in their natural habitat, and 'remembering' them in my heart.

"Yes! Such are the precious opportunities to 'aid in service to all Life Forms' (one of the purposes of the TRTAI) through the marine mammals and the use of The Radiance Technique. These animals have expanded and continue here-now to expand within me the knowingness of True Service and True Inner-Connection to and for Life in all its magnificent forms here on Earth."

Crystal Sierra
The Fifth Degree
Florida

There is a nationally known sanctuary in Florida that began as the outgrowth of basically one human's concern for wildlife. Ralph Heath founded the Suncoast Seabird Sanctuary and has brought the brown pelican, once an endangered species, back by simply rescuing the brown pelicans that have been injured by fishers and others, caring for them and supporting them to mate in captivity. He has now taken their thriving numbers to begin a repopulation of the species. His Gulf Coast location in Florida has a fly-in during cold weather when pelicans hover nearby when the natural food supply grows slim, awaiting the food the volunteers at the Sanctuary feed them. Animals have an unspoken communication with one another and evidently can share the location where there are loving, food-sharing caretakers.

One of my more unusual encounters occurred while walking along the Gulf Beaches near the water with a friend. We saw at

a slight distance a large white egret with a bloody and droop-
ing wing standing and moving slowly along the beach. These
graceful birds are beautiful to watch. I had never wanted to
come closer to one before, yet seeing its injury, I wanted to help.
In this instance, hands-on seemed out of the question.

I sent my friend to call the Suncoast Seabird Sanctuary
which was nearby and I stayed with the egret. I held my hands
toward it and although it did not back away from me, its
injuries seemed serious and painful. I decided to use the Cosmic Symbols and began directing the harmless, and universal
energy of TRT toward the egret, creating the Cosmic Symbols
moving through its body.

We began a quiet "walk" down the beach. I could see the bird
clearly and the wing was very bloody and torn with a large
fishhook dangling from it still on a fisher's wire and line. It
could walk easily and seemed alert and aware of me. The bird
moved ahead of me at a slow pace, calm and unafraid. I moved
along at a distance of only two to three feet from it, continuing
my radiant energy directing. We went about a half a mile or so
down the beach and I decided we might need to return to our
original location so the helpers from the Seabird Sanctuary
could find us. I used our inner-connection with the Cosmic
Symbols to help us turn around. I got ahead of the bird, using
the Cosmic Symbols to support our "communication" and
began walking toward it. It turned and moved back down the
beach toward where we had begun.

I was truly at peace and feeling very at one with this beautiful bird. I felt its serenity and its natural trust of me. Seeing its
injuries, I could have been jangled or fearful myself, yet using
the Cosmic Symbols and focusing my attention on directing
energy kept me calm and supportive without any "thoughts" or
fears moving through me. I was unaware of time or of anything
other than the bird, the symbols and our inner communication.

My friend returned with Ralph Heath and he "captured" the
bird easily, remarking that sometimes it is hard for people to
approach them when they are injured. The bird was taken to
the Sanctuary for examination, surgery and rehabilitation.
The whole incident probably took no more than an hour but it
left an indelible memory within me of oneness and of an ability
to "touch" with energy a living creature. I had supported this
bird and communicated with it effortlessly for an hour even
though I could not at that moment touch it with my hands. The
use of The Radiance Technique is empowering every day of my

life. This incident lives in my heart as one of the first times I knew the radiant power of inner communication and inner "touch" with a non-domesticated animal.

Organizations with services similar to those we have shared spring up in communities with different kinds of animals, because humans become interested in helping. You can use your radiant energy to connect with any of these services and support their outreach. Please see Chapter 8,"Resources Worldwide," for more contacts with those supporting animals in different ways around the globe.

One of the unique aspects of The Radiance Technique® is that it provides a connection for vital, Light-energy which can be used creatively, efficiently and harmlessly, and adapted to any situation by the person with the "touch of radiance."

Barbara Ray, Ph.D.

CHAPTER FIVE

ADOPTING AN ANIMAL FRIEND

When you adopt an animal friend to live in your home, you are beginning an energy relationship and the use of The Radiance Technique® serves both of you supportively and harmlessly. Many possibilities exist for applying radiant energy from the moment you have the thought to bring an animal friend into your life.

In selecting an animal for adoption, use your hands-on first with yourself. Plan your adoption carefully, making sure that your lifestyle will support the animal as well as yourself. Remember to look into the time you will have available to train and educate and relate to a new energy and new life within your home. Make sure you know the species and its needs and whether they can be met. Many different kinds of animals can join your household and all will benefit from your use of The Radiance Technique® with them.

You can begin with the Discovery Exercise in *The Official Handbook of The Radiance Technique*® called "The Polarity Exercise." When you have a choice to make, you can place one animal in your Heart Center under one radiant hand and another animal under the other radiant hand. Then bring your attention to your radiant heart hands. Supported by universal energy, take turns becoming aware of the animal of first your right hand and then your left. Go back and forth allowing yourself to explore all you like, or dislike about the particular animal. Proceed with the whole exercise exploring your "likes and dislikes" or the "pros and cons" of your decision, allowing yourself a half hour or more to fully explore and discover your choice.

It is very helpful to write down how you feel right after you do this exercise and to note your "pros and cons". Then, when you do the Polarity Exercise at another time, you can notice how you are changing or how you seem to be confirming a certain choice. You may even want to do this several times as you become more deeply aware of all of your feelings as you discover your choice. This exercise can also be done if you are choosing between animals such as deciding whether you wish to adopt a puppy or a kitten. Use the Polarity Exercise to choose between like animals such as between two kittens, or between two puppies or two birds.

The following sharing gives you a deeper look at the adoption process shared when this student began her process for bringing a cat into her home:

"On September 1, 1987, a cat and I mutually adopted one another at the Humane Society in Topeka, Kan. It was a difficult process for me to go to the Humane Society in the first place as I felt so sorry for the animals there but I was determined to assist one animal's cycle by adopting it. I utilized The First and The Second Degrees of The Radiance Technique® prior to going to the Humane Society over the course of several days to help prepare myself emotionally and intellectually and to direct energy to the animals. As I drove to the Humane Society, I continued to direct and utilized The Second Degree during every moment. I spent two hours on my first visit and another two hours during my second visit.

"During my visits, I would interact with each animal in every cage. No matter what the condition of the animal, whether friendly or scared or confused or whatever, they each, in turn, would respond to me. I would pattern the symbols on their foreheads and I would touch their heart centers and their paws. I would direct energy and interact with each of them. Each animal for that brief contact would respond to The Radiance Technique® and the light in their eyes would seem to be enhanced. Each animal for that brief moment of interaction would seem to relax and be more at peace.

"During my first visit, I met the cat being whom I would later adopt. The cat was at the back of the cage and when I approached and spoke softly to it, it immediately came to the front of the cage. We interacted for several minutes. As

I already mentioned, it seemed as if he and I were mutually adopting one another. An employee of the Humane Society walked by me and I asked if I might hold the cat (not realizing that my request was against the rules). The employee said, 'Yes.' and opened the cage door and picked up the cat and gave him to me. (It is an important point to mention that the employee also closed the door to the cage at this time.)

"At the moment I first held Strider, we 'connected.' I held him against my Heart Center and he relaxed completely against me. Within a second or two, as I was adjusting to him and he to me, a terrible racket began as two dogs started fighting. The employee left us to see what had happened. At that moment, I realized that I was holding a strange animal and that the noise and the reactions from the other animals could frighten the cat (not declawed) and he could, in turn, hurt me without that intention. I continued utilizing The Second Degree and patterning and remained calm within myself; I remained centered and balanced. Much to my surprise and relief, the cat remained calm, his entire body in a relaxed state, he was alert and curious as to what was going on. I continued to hold him for at least five minutes with great confusion going on around us.

"By that time, several employees were involved, the fight had subsided, and things were returning to normal. The manager of the Humane Society noticed that I was holding a cat and immediately ordered an employee to 'get that cat back in a cage!' The manager continued, 'That woman should not be holding a cat! She could be hurt!!' So, an employee took the cat away from me and put it back in the cage.

"At our separation, the cat became upset and went immediately to the back of the cage with its back to me. It acted in a depressed state. When I spoke to it, it would not respond. I could not coax it to turn around or to respond to me. The contrast between the past ten minutes and the present moment were startling and vivid. It seemed as if our connection was broken.

"I was presently asked if I had found an animal that I would like to adopt and I said yes. I said that I wanted to adopt the cat and the employee was pleased and went to being work on the adoption papers. Within minutes, she returned to tell me that the cat had just been brought in that morning and legally I could not adopt the cat until 72 hours had passed and since that time frame was over the weekend, it would actually be four days. I was horrified! I asked if there was anything I could do and naturally, there wasn't.

"All I could do was put my name down for the cat and return within four days. The cat was so depressed by this time that I spent some time with it, reassuring it that I would return, that I would direct energy to it and support it. As slowly as the four days passed, they did and I went to the Humane Society to adopt the cat at the first opportunity. When I returned to the place, I went to him and he responded once again immediately and seemed to reflect outwardly the work I had done on the inner planes. Since there are many papers to fill out and the process takes some time, I worked with the other animals while I waited. I would continually physically return to the cat and reassure him and direct energy to him. In short order, the adoption was completed and I could leave with my new friend.

"I named the cat being Strider (stride through the gateways), the name given to a special character in "The Hobbit" series written by J.R.R. Tolkien. The Humane Society Manager did not know for certain Strider's age, estimating him to be approximately one year old.

SUPPORTING THE ADOPTION PROCESS
WITH RADIANT ENERGY

"The first few weeks that we lived together, I could tell that Strider had been well cared for and had been loved by his previous owner. In addition, Strider was an alert and bright cat, but he did not seem to know how to 'play.'

"As required by the Humane Society, I had Strider neutered. According to the 'experts' on cats, I have to believe it is ultimately an act of love and kindness. I did **not** have him declawed as I believe one can teach a cat not to claw inappropriately. Also, Strider was taken to the vet for his shots and to remedy the problem of worms.

"Before taking him to the vet, I would spend time with him with hands-on and patterning. I would direct energy while driving Strider to the vet and I would repeat affirmations out loud. I directed energy on the one occasion

Strider had to stay at the vet's for 5-6 hours. After returning home, I would spend time with Strider, with hands-on and patterning. Over the course of those visits, Strider responded immediately to The Radiance Technique® in supporting his healing or normalizing process.

"During the first weeks, months and year that Strider lived with me, I interacted with him on a daily basis with The Radiance Technique®. For instance, Strider would join me while I was involved with hands-on. I would then place my hands on him for 20-30 minutes at a time! He would respond to the hands-on sessions by a deep settling down, complete physical relaxation with mental alertness, and eventually he would drift off into deep sleep and rest. On several occasions I would continue hands-on sessions with Strider for one hour or as long as two hours!

"Also during our first year together, I would engage Strider in 'play.' I would teach him new games and allow him to discover the pleasure in play. I played with him every morning, afternoon an evening for extended periods of time. At this juncture, Strider is as playful as a kitten; his entire demeanor changes during play. His face transforms into a kitten's face and he is tireless in his energy and joy in the games of discovery and pouncing that we engage in. My friends and family have commented on the changes in him over the past two years in the area of play. Strider seems to transcend age and time when he plays. He is once again the kitten he was or could have been. He is radiantly involved and he enjoys the moments intensely.

"In addition, during the first year that I had him, he was cautious and unsure of visitors. He now readily greets people and is not afraid. Strider, in fact, extends his welcome to all who may enter 'our' apartment. He is sociable, outgoing and warm."

JoJean Ewart, Ph.D.
The Radiant Third Degree
Washington

In addition to that sharing, one that involved a Siamese named Ray Ray also shows the importance of hands-on in developing latent or undeveloped relationships. Ray Ray had a very difficult early life, having been in a home that was robbed. He became very terrorized by that incident as a young kitten.

He withdrew, became very cautious with humans and avoided contact.

Later his life involved a number of animals in the same household including a dog as well as two or three other cats. By then, Ray Ray was very wary and did not relate to humans very well at all. When his caretaker moved to another city, he was left for several weeks in an empty house with very little furniture and no companion, human or animal.

A part-time caretaker discovered that he was retreating more and more and seemed to be falling ill from lack of contact. He was immediately adopted by radiant friends who nursed him back to health. Ray Ray was about six years old at this time and had never been very close with humans.

Fortunately, he was suffering no organic illness when he was adopted to live with his new caretaker, Fred. W. Wright, who has studied to The Fourth Degree. However, he was still withdrawn and did not approach humans. He would run and hide when approached. In Fred's home, he was touched constantly with radiant hands even though at first he ran and hid from such friendly overtures. He was also picked up *every day* and held and petted. He had never to that time been a "lap" cat, not in his whole life. And, he had never purred when touched or picked up. It took several months of consistent loving and radiant attention for him to become, indeed, a "lap" cat who now climbs into Fred's lap and loves to sit for hours, purring, enjoying hands-on and sleeping there peacefully. He eagerly awaits these opportunities for bonding.

It is important to point out that consistent use of radiant hands-on can help an animal on many levels. Ray Ray is an example that even after years of retreating behavior, an animal can form a bond with humans who are consistent and loving. He is still not as gregarious as he might have been with a different history, yet he loves radiant touch and to be in a radiant lap! His purr attests to that.

Animals of all species need the radiance of your hands whenever possible. Birds respond enthusiastically to touching or radiant "massage." The following example delightfully describes a loving relationship with a parrot:

"I acquired a young 6-month-old African Grey parrot. I named him 'Hero,' although the name was a more apt description of what his personality might become rather than his present one. Hero was said to be hand-fed from

69

birth and tame. But, he was also very shy and awkward—like a young child just beginning to find his way.

"From the beginning of our relationship, I have made a practice of giving my feathered friend radiant energy—first via the Attunement that I learned at The Third Degree (3A) and using the Cosmic Symbols that I learned in The Second Degree; then through a surprising turn of events, direct hands-on transmission of energy.

"One day, I put my arms in a circle on the top of Hero's cage as he was taking a little 'constitutional.' He moved into my encircling arms through an opening made between my hands and buried his head into my elbow. Instinctively, I began to stroke and even to massage him from head to tail in a firm steady rhythm with a loving touch. Hero stayed in my arms seeming to say 'More, please, more!'

"Then one evening I took him from my shoulder and put him into my lap. He protested at first, but then appeared very contented as I began to give him a radiant massage. And this practice has continue.

"The first weeks and months of our burgeoning friendship were absorbing and full of surprises. There was never a dull moment as Hero began to trust me more and more—as he started to come to my hand and climb onto my shoulders, drink from my breakfast glass of juice, and delicately take from my mouth crumbs or toast. And what a joy to hear his first words: 'Hello, Hero' and then 'I love you.'

"While most parrots, I was told, are supposed to make nuisance noises from time to time, Hero is an exception. I have never heard a strident noise from him. Only spiraling whistles and songs and a slowly expanding vocabulary.

"He is truly a radiant bird—and possibly a unique one. Could it be that he is the only bird on this planet who receives regular Radiant energy massages?"

This wonderful sharing has a very interesting addition that happened. Time had passed and the caretaker had expanded Hero's vocabulary to include such loving favorites as "Good morning sweetheart. You are gorgeous! I love you, Joe. I love you Hero. You are something. Don't you bite! Good boy . . . pretty bird." And he also whistled "a sometimes accurate and sometimes inaccurate version of Yankee Doodle Dandy and loved to improvise melodies of his own." Then, his caretaker had to take an exceptionally long trip:

"I travel quite often, and when I do some bird-loving friends take care of Hero. Recently, when I was about to go abroad for six weeks, I received the unfortunate news that my friends' birds (finches and canaries) had come down with an infection. Of course, I did not dare to give Hero over to them. Eventually, I found a man who was in charge of the bird department of a well-known local pet store who agreed to 'board' Hero in his home where he had other birds. I left on my travels relieved and happy to have found such a knowledgeable, experienced person to parrot sit.

"Six weeks later when I picked up Hero and took him home I was shocked to find that his energy had changed considerably. Instead of being soft and gentle, he was now harsh and strident, emitting shrill angry whistles and other unpleasant sounds. What had occurred that had changed Hero so drastically? I would never know, but I did know that I could not live with a bird that had such negative energy. I was ready to part with my former beloved pet. 'But, wait,' I reminded myself, 'you have a remarkable tool, The Radiance Technique, to try to bring Hero back to his more loving, more humorous self.'

"Thus began a fascinating project whereby I 'worked' with Hero every day, with appropriate Cosmic Symbols and the Attunement Process to affect a change in his energy. Gradually over the next month or so a transformation of Hero did take place. What a joy it was to see my beloved bird move from dark density to a place again of laughter (literally!) and light. Not a day goes by now that Hero does not receive his morning Attunement and how he enjoys his daily bath of light. And I am happy to add that at this writing he is learning the opening measures of the first movement of Beethoven's Fifth Symphony.

"Recently, I have been interacting with Hero in another profound way. African Gray Parrots are apt to be threatened if you reach your hands directly towards them and they may bite you as a result.

"However, one day I began to spiral energy towards him, softly, gently, weaving a web of cosmic energy until finally spiraling directly–touching–his Heart Center. He seemed surprised at this new experience with a sense of wonder as I continued to spiral/touch his Heart Center. I have communicated with Hero like this several more

71

times and know that we now have another way of bonding from our inner hearts."

Joseph Gifford
The Fifth Degree
Massachusetts

An important aspect of inviting a new animal into your home is to be sure of what the relationships are with any animals already in the home, or to see your purposes for adoption of a single animal more clearly. A look at your own past relation ships with animals can be a vital growth experience, giving you a clearer perspective for the new arrival in your home. A discovery exercise was published in the ongoing column in *The Radiance Technique Journal* dedicated to sharings and information about TRT and animals of all kinds. First, find a time that you can set aside for this discovery process, spending time with hands-on meditation. It is very helpful to have a specific time set aside whether it is ten minutes or a half an hour just for this purpose. It is also an important exercise that you might want to make notes about, writing the experience in a personal awareness journal–perhaps, an "Animals and Me" journal. When you complete the exercise, just write down your feelings or the things that came up for you without making any judgment or evaluation of them. Then, each time you do the exercise, add to your notes to capture your feelings just as they are.

Begin by placing your hands in your Heart Center (Front Position #1). Using your radiant touch to support you, focus on the first animal you can remember as a member of your family's household. Allow yourself to become fully involved in the process of remembering and being with that particular animal, bringing it into your heart in the present. If you have studied The Second Degree or beyond, you can use your hands in your heart while using the Cosmic Symbols and/or directing energy to the animal and completing an *inner* hands-on with its energy field. If you have studied to The Third Degree (3A) or beyond, you may choose to give the animal an Attunement and then to continue directing energy to it. You can explore several animals that you have known in each session or use the time for just one animal to be fully aware of. Following is a sharing from one student who has done this exercise over a period of time to be in radiant touch with the animals she has known:

"I use my Heart Center and image each animal in my Heart Center, using radiant touch after I have completed an Attunement. I set my timer so that I can have at least seven minutes and I continue this exercise over a period of days as I can find the time.

"I was surprised by how vivid and alive the past is from this point of clarity, i.e. the universal energy accessed as you do the exercise. What I experienced was not from a point of emotion, although much of my past experience with animals was from that point.

"One animal that I had entirely forgotten came into my awareness as well as the unusual circumstances surrounding how it came to be in my family. Thirty-five years had elapsed since that animal had lived with us and yet how clearly some images were and how alive!

"With one animal, using the attunements and my Heart Center, I experienced an emotional release through a flood of tears–but without any grief, sadness or the normal emotions experienced with crying."

Yesnie Carrington
The Fifth Degree
Florida

You can use this discovery exercise as a meditation to explore animals you may be wanting to adopt into your home, or as you welcome one into your home, benefiting from your past experiences to grow and explore new relationships with animals. Your deepening awareness of animals may support you to go beyond your own emotional needs to create a different more expanded relationship with the next animal you invite into your household.

ADDING ANOTHER ANIMAL WHERE ANOTHER ANIMAL ALREADY LIVES

When you adopt or bring a new animal into your home, your hands-on and your directing of energy to the Heart Centers is very important. Each animal, a dog meeting a cat, or an animal meeting its own kind, needs the gentle and persistent support of radiant energy. The following sharing emphasizes the importance of being persistent:

"I have two radiant kitty beings in my home; Loretti (the Coal Miner's Kitty) has lived with me for almost five years and Dendur (Lion) for nearly two. When Dendur first arrived on the scene, there was a lot of kitty tension and general not getting along . . . these two wouldn't even sleep in the same room together! I fretted some, and began to incorporate them into my directing of energy during the High Noon Networking. This improved their inter-cat-nectedness–at least they would be in the same room together. Still, they were wary of one another.

"One afternoon when lying on the bed, I took Dendur over to her side (protesting all the way) and knelt between them, placing one of my hands on each of their kittyheart centers in a kittyheartmeld. They looked at me like I was out of my human mind, taking all this in for a moment or two. Little by little during the following days, we expanded on this until they would lay there for a full minute and more–a kittyeternity to these two!

"They began playing together, sleeping on the same piece of furniture, and now are wonder-full kittyfriends.

"I now work with their li'l kittyheart centers regularly, giving them heartkisses, too. If I forget their kittyheart sessions, they let me know!"

Shannon Orrock
The Fourth Degree
California

Sometimes a new animal added to the home needs special attention and care. With TRT you can support it immediately. A student shares the importance of TRT in integrating an abused cat into her home and how TRT helps support change in the animal's life:

"Our beautiful, blue-eyed, long-haired white cat was rescued from someone who had abused her. When we got her, she walked in a crouch, shook, hid under furniture and was terrified by any sounds.

"I began by directing Cosmic Symbols to her and directing energy as I had learned at The Second Degree. Eventually, she let me put my hands on her for short periods of time. This cat is now the most outgoing (of five) in the family. She follows the vacuum cleaner, plays chase with the dog and greets all our guests."

Jo-Ann Benit
The Second Degree
Louisiana

GETTING TO KNOW EACH OTHER
WITH RADIANT SUPPORT

When adding a new animal into the home, allow the animals to have a space of their own within the home for a few days or a week if at all possible. Spend extra time with each animal as the new one's scent or sound is being noticed by the former "only" animal friend who was first resident. They will make their usual territorial comments to one another, hissing, barking, chirping, smelling at the door where the other is, stalking nearby—each according to its species. Give them time for these displays. It will help you to know about each animal's habits before you introduce them so that you are not surprised by the intensity they can bring to a first encounter.

Use your hands-on with each animal either through radiant touch or simply near the level of touch depending on the response. Make sure that food intake, sleep and individual attention is given to each one. You are building a supportive energy for them to come together in. If you have studied to The Second Degree or beyond, create a cosmic cocoon of loving and spiralling energy each day to embrace each animal as you direct universal energy to them. Keep their Heart Centers in your awareness and direct to their loving capacities.

When you choose to bring them together, be unobtrusive. Let them sniff or stare or stalk or slink by each other as they choose. Animals are very inventive in staking out each other. They know another animal is in the house before you've even thought of everything you want to do to make them aware. Your best support is to create a sustaining and harmless energy to embrace their initial meeting. Let your expectations go and just watch and direct your loving energy to the encounter. It may take a short or long duration and you may choose to keep them separate for eating or sleeping or other reasons as you gradually integrate their lives with one another.

In the following sharing, the integration of a new kitten into the household was radiantly supported by the caretaker and her network of friends:

"In early November I met a beautiful little Siamese kitten that I wanted to bring into my home.

"Having an older cat—and being aware that 'cat people' recommend at least a week of separation in different rooms when introducing a new cat into a household with an existing cat—I began daily to do Attunements and to direct radiant energy to each and to both little felines for about five days before bringing her home.

"A network of people also were directing energy on a daily basis to them. I did hands-on with Flower Face (the older cat already at home with me) and told her how great it would be for her to have another kitty friend to play with and to love, and to keep her company when I was away.

"Starlight came home with me in a kitty carrier, and I placed the cage in the middle of the living room floor and sat down beside her. Flower Face circled the cage and growled, peering inside at the cowering little one.

"Speaking gently to both of them, I again attuned and directed energy to them. Flower Face stopped growling and began rubbing against me. I held her in my lap, doing hands-on and assuring her that I loved her dearly and that Starlight had come to be with both of us.

"Starlight spent the night in the bathroom as a protective measure, and Flower Face cuddled closely that night as I continued attuning the relationship between them. At 3 a.m., Starlight woke me mewing quite loudly.

"I went into the bathroom, sat on the floor and held her in my Heart Center, doing hands-on for several minutes. I placed a T-shirt I had been wearing in her bed, put her down, did a few more minutes of hands-on, and she went back to sleep till morning.

"When we awoke, I let Starlight out to explore the house, leaving Flower Face closed in the bedroom. After a while, I opened the door and Flower Face growled and hissed while Starlight jumped around her and cowered at the older cat's growling.

"I watched and continued to direct radiant energy as they interacted together. I kept the new little one in the bathroom that day while I was working and kept attuning and directing energy. When I got home, they both mewed and purred, welcoming me home.

"I let Starlight out, and after a few minutes of Flower Face growling, sniffing, making a few swats at the new Siamese kitten and getting acquainted, off they ran together, chasing through the house. In an ordinary sense, this was an amazing event—just 24 hours after I brought the new kitten home, they were romping and playing together.

"What a joy to direct the unconditional, loving energy of The Radiance Technique® and to watch the cats as they experience and express that energy in their lives. They are very loving cats, to me and to each other. They sometimes sit on my lap all wrapped around each other, purring their love and contentment.

"They are now the best of friends, playing, jostling, chasing one another, sleeping together and wrapped up together, and often they do paws-on with each other. Yes, of course, they both have been attuned to The Radiance Technique.® Celebration!"

Marilyn-Rose Alvey
The Fifth Degree
Florida

When I brought a new Siamese kitten into a household with two other six-months-old cats, I began by having them in different rooms but able to see or sniff each other. I did hands-on with each of them throughout the day, directed energy to their Heart Centers, and talked back and forth with them, letting the domestic kittens "hear" the voice of the Siamese. They quickly began to play "paws under the door" with each other and got used to the new smells of one another. Within a few days, I let the older kittens see the baby without a door but in a small protected cage enclosure. As soon as I took the new kitten out and handed her to the male to sniff, he began to lick her and both began to purr. The exact same behavior occurred with the female cat. I let her sniff and lick the baby. These three were close immediately with the male even allowing the baby to suckle his warm tummy even though he had no milk to give. They all are one family and play and sleep together as if they had always known one another.

Once integrated, many animals become fast friends with species quite different from their own. They will be enhancing your education as well as you learn to see their behaviors as very different from that of humans. Read the entries in *The Expanded Reference Manual* under "Observer" and "Discovery Process" and keep your own journal such as an "Adoption Journal" or an "Animals and Me Journal" to remind yourself of the different stages of development that occur with the animal or animals in your home. It is one of the joys of life that humans and animals of an infinite variety—all very different—can live together harmoniously. As humans, it is important to remember that we have a genuine responsibility for developing ourselves into radiant caretakers for the animal kingdom.

CHAPTER SIX

THE DEATH AND DYING PROCESS WITH ANIMALS

There is no more important way for you to use TRT than in the support of yourself and your pet or animal friend in the death and dying process. You bring a universal and harmless support as you share radiant energy with them when you use TRT. In this section we explore the radiant release from powerlessness that many alumni have actually experienced as they used TRT in the dying process with their animal friends.

Many alumni have written to us that with TRT, the death and dying process of animals is often experienced joyously, as a deep inner contact is sustained beyond the dying process. That this chapter is full of joy and gratitude is not a surprise. These sharings are the tangible testimony of experiences and discoveries shared with love.

In *The Expanded Reference Manual*, Dr. Ray has a beautiful entry concerning the aspects of Life that coexist in the cycles of birthing and dying. She writes about the "Death and Dying Process," on page 29. With her permission we are reprinting a portion of it:

"One of the most important of our Life processes is that of dying. Life is the whole: birthing and dying are cycles—are polarities manifesting in different degrees and aspects within the Whole of Universal Life. . . . With The Radiance Technique, you can always consciously apply universal energy to yourself in any stage of any birthing dying process you are experiencing. With others—people, pets, plants, situations, the Earth—you can give harmless, universal, radiant support. You can learn to help yourself

78

and others in the birthing dying process both of which are extremely significant transition periods in a lifetime. With TRT it would be possible to go though this process without fear, without attachment and in full consciousness fully awakened."

As caretakers of animals, humans often must make the decision that determines the time of death for pets. Using TRT helps them make what might otherwise be very difficult decisions. And, using the radiant, harmless and sustaining energy of The Radiance Technique, they support themselves as well as their pets through the process. Following is a sharing from a student of The Second Degree:

"My most meaningful experience was easily using TRT to help my cat in her final illness. I loved her more than any pet I've ever had and she was with me for 18 years. When I completed my seminar she had kidney failure and was already in the process of dying. I was in a state of grief and continual migraine headaches. Using The Radiance Technique cleared my headaches and freed me to give her my full attention. She was on subcutaneous fluids which would restore her for about three days and then she would become nauseous and dehydrated. I decided to have her euthanized to spare her worse pain and further breakdown. We set a date with the vet. The night before I shared the hands-on application with her. She became incredibly hot, as did I, began to purr intensely and her eyes lighted up. Then she was seized by muscle spasms from her head to her tail—in traveling waves. The next morning was the date of her euthanasia and when I awoke, she was sitting on the window sill with her head thrown back sniffing the fresh air and radiating pleasure and happiness. I called the vet and he said to wait until the next day. Meanwhile Bunny had one beautiful, happy day to go out and inspect the neighbors' garbage in the back hall, hide pencils under the rug and do all of her favorite things which she hadn't been capable of for weeks. The night before her euthanasia, I slept with my hands around her. Gary took her for the injection and held her. I don't think I'm more thankful for any one thing The Radiance Technique has blessed me with than this gentle passing and profound closeness I had with this beloved pet."

Lorrie Glaze
The Second Degree
New York

Feelings of helplessness and sadness are entirely different when experienced through the supportive use of The Radiance Technique. The dying process is, as these sharings show, a profound experience for everyone involved with the animal. Following are several sharings where more than one radiant being aided in creating an "unforgettable experience:"

"Our beautiful Irish Setter, 'Kelly Erin O'Zuhl,' made her transition in July at the age of 13 years and 3 months. Wilma Nichols, our close family friend who has studied to The Fourth Degree of TRT, was so helpful during Kelly's final days and in preparing her and me for the transition.

"Each time she would enter our home, Kelly would become quiet and look forward eagerly to the attunement she knew she would receive. In addition, I carried on daily hands-on sessions with her for several months. Kelly responded well and came to me first thing in the morning—and again at night. Since we live in a two-story house, many times her legs would fail her when she climbed the stairs. After I sat beside her and calmed her with The Radiance Technique, she could continue up the stairs with me. Our veterinarian could not believe that she was doing this in her physical condition.

"I am confident that the transition was easy for her. Her final farewell was a gentle tapping of her tail on the living room floor. Wilma also helped make the sad news more bearable for my husband and son who were not at home at the time.

"It was a very special attunement during one of our beautiful sunsets that Wilma gave me while I held the container with Kelly's ashes. It was an unforgettable experience for both of us."

Eloise Zuhl
The Second Degree
Arizona

Another student shares some of her life of hands-on with her dog and some of the interesting benefits for him. She also found a great sense of freedom when this well-loved companion made his transition:

"Ever since studying the First Degree of The Radiance Technique® one of my greatest joys has been the application of hands-on—with myself and sharing it with others.

80

With each additional degree the energy grows and expands.

"My Yorkshire terriers benefited tremendously–their veterinarian would be the first to agree. My eldest, Stoney, had a history of intestinal problems and early, very early, one morning I heard the unmistakable gurgles of an attack coming on. It would be four hours before I could take him to the vet. So, I held him and did hands-on, all the time attuning him and doing the symbols. Three hours later, no gurgles and a *very* relaxed and happy little dog.

"He was 14 years old and had lost all the hair on his back, not from skin disease, simply from 'old age'. About three weeks after our 'early morning' of hands-on, I noticed he had started to grow a new coat of hair. It was time for a check-up and I asked the vet if he had ever seen an older dog grow a new coat and he responded: 'Never–I don't know what you are doing, but *keep on doing it.*'

"A number of years later, Stoney's health had greatly deteriorated. He had been in the hospital (the same veterinarian) for over a week and was basically being sustained by a daily injection and then he would sleep. Dr. Lynch and I spoke and we both realized that the time had come to 'let him go.' He reassured me that Stoney was so accustomed to the daily injection that it would not be frightening for him.

"I called those closest to me for networking for Stoney, for me and for the vet. I then started doing Attunements and began to cry. I kept going with the symbols and there was a tremendous spiraling of energies. I started crying for myself and how much I would miss him. Then the energy turned, and the tears were of joy for his freedom. It set me free as well."

Demeter Sierra
The Fifth Degree
Florida

This sharing describes a really heart-filled time of preparation for the transition of a beloved animal:

"Benjamin was a 13-year-old male Black Labrador mix, and he was very arthritic throughout his body, and incontinent. I applied TRT to Benjamin and to his human caretaker the week before his transition.

81

"We sang to him: 'Listen, listen, listen to my heartsong,' while doing the heart meld between him and (his caretaker). He rested his chin peacefully on the triangle of our arms. While he was always loving and affectionate.., Benjamin was a dog who showed it with touch, instead of dog kisses. During the song and heart meld, he suddenly lifted his head and kissed me.

"The following Saturday was his transition, and the same sequence of events as above occurred again. He comforted my friend in her sadness about his leaving by touching her with his paw. His eyes shone and he was calm and peaceful during those last hours before his transition."

Jeri Ryan
The Third Degree (3A)
California

The profound bonds of friendship with animals expand the heart and enhance the human capacity for love. In the following sharing, a sense of inner communication had been well developed between the human and cat as friends and this special form of communication supports both of them as the cat moves through her dying process:

"A couple of days preceding her transcendence, my 14-year-old, First Degree, Siamese cat 'Pushpa' had ceased to eat and drink, but despite her physical weakness communicated to me that she needed a lot of stroking and hands-on. I also kept a candle lit for her day and night. In the past she often sat on my lap while I mediated and did my hands-on or directing of energy, and when I wasn't sitting in my 'Attunement chair' she used to sit in it anyway!

"I tried to stroke her, but she pushed me gently away with her Radiant front paws. She would always seek out a sunny patch to lie in, so I sat for hours in the sun, one hand under her head, the other stroking and holding her velvety front paws in the palm of my hand. When I left her for just a few minutes, her paws would reach out searching the air for me, and I responded touching them and telling her reassuringly that I was there.

"When she started to twitch, I knew that her soul was starting to leave her body and several times I saw her legs moving as though she were running. I wondered if she was running away from something or making haste down the long dark tunnel toward the Light. Despite a dense, heavy atmosphere in the room, there was a great sense of Inner Peace. How grateful I am that she chose . . . to 'go' in the safety and support of my arms. I projected Cosmic Symbols to/for her throughout the next day . . . so she could take that energy with her on her journey."

Susan Howell
The Fourth Degree
England

For those involved in the following events, the process for the animal was also an opportunity for growth for the humans as well as they met together in radiant Celebration:

CELEBRATION AND GRATITUDE

"A friend of mine had a severely ill male cat named Gandhi, who's health had been deteriorating rapidly due to a severe bladder malfunction. After much heart-full processing, she decided that the right course of support would be to put him 'to sleep' through veterinary injection.

"My friend invited me to be present during the process. I was honored to participate in Gandhi's transition, as he was a harmless, loving animal who had been the first cat I had ever responded to without fear. Other people had also shared with me that Gandhi was one of the most gentle and affectionate cats they had ever known.

"At the time, I lived in another city from my friend, so I took a plane and arrived the day before Gandhi was to go to the vet. He greeted me at the front door, a thin little cat with hardly any vital life energy–yet radiating a sweet, loving presence. His body was very cold and he didn't have much physical strength. My friend had invited two other people over to be with Gandhi his last night, and there was no sadness among us. In fact, we had a small 'birthday' party complete with pizza. One of my favorite images of Gandhi is from that night, as he lay spread out on top of the warm pizza box, in the center of a circle of his human friends.

"I had been continually directing energy through the use of the Cosmic Symbols and Attunements to Gandhi, his sister cat Saqqara and my friend. Also, much hands-on was exchanged and again, I was aware of how little physical energy he had left in his body. He would respond by talking and purring, rubbing softly against my hands.

"The next morning was truly Gandhi's birthday! He was alert and talkative as we drove to the vet hospital. Three radiant human beings and one very radiant cat arrived in an energy of spiraling celebration. We all wore white shirts with bright yellow suns on our hearts, and Gandhi was carried in a radiant sun hand towel, his blue eyes shining.

"As we waited for the vet in one of the examining rooms, Gandhi was calm and purring. Each one of us spoke with him, and I thanked him for being in, and expanding, my life. I put one hand on my heart and one on his and we shared in a precious heart meld of energy.

"The vet entered and remarked on our shirts, Gandhi's towel, and that it 'felt good' in the room. He asked if we were 'ready,' and my friend held Gandhi in preparation for his injection.

"This was the first death experience I had ever been present for, human or animal, and the moment of energy release from the physical form is one I shall always remember. As Gandhi's body slumped, I became aware that it was just his body that was 'dead'. Gandhi was still very much present in the room. As the vet left us all alone, we all put our hands on Gandhi's body and I began to experience a heat and fire like I had never known. I began to sweat intensely, as did the others, and it was literally hard to keep my hands on Gandhi's form. I kept directing Cosmic Symbols as the fire of Gandhi's energy field was expanding up, out, and around his little body on the table. My heart was full of joy and tears of gratitude fell. The three of us spoke about the fire present in those eternal moments of transition, and I knew then that we were helping to 'birth' Gandhi into a new cycle of being, a different expression of energy. I experienced the life/fire that is born out of death, and knew that, through The Radiance Technique, I was able to touch the 'inner Gandhi.'

84

"That true flame of Gandhi's being lives in my heart today and everyday I choose to Remember–his death was/ is outside of time and space."

Crystal Sierra
The Fifth Degree
Florida

In my own life, I had an experience with the dying process last year that was and is a joyous and tender remembering for me. I felt so supported and so did my longtime friend and companion, a wonderful "calico" or tri-colored cat named Lady Olympia, "Oly" to many who knew her. Her deep green eyes had taken many of us on a journey of the heart for she was a very special being. She had lived with me for about eight years or so. In her lifetime, she had the opportunity to live with several radiant beings, the first of whom was Dr. Barbara Ray. Her life had begun with radiance and support and she traveled with Dr. Ray across the country in her early life. Some of her first years were thus spent outdoors. Yet, later in her life, she became an indoor "only" cat, a position she cherished. In her unusual life, she had lived with various other cats, at least two different dogs and sometimes several animals in the household, always a household in which TRT was a way of life.

A real healer herself, she had been attuned by Dr. Ray while still a young cat and did "paws-on" with humans as well as loving the hands-on for herself. She could spend hours in my lap enjoying the sharing of energy, and she loved to sleep on or against the human she shared her home with. (Lucky me!) She was a unique and gentle cat who was physically small and throughout her life looked like a "kitten", instead of a mature cat of some years. She was a friend to many in her younger times as she posed for one of the first Handbooks to demonstrate the hands-on with animals. (We called her the centerfold kitty.) She is also remembered by a close human friend on whom she placed her paws when my friend was near death from cancer, the surgery that had been done to remove it, and the radiation she had undergone. This friend was being helped by Dr. Ray in her healing process through what she called her own "near-death" experience. She vividly remembers receiving hours and hours of hands-on, and at night Oly would do paws-on with her as well. She has eternal gratitude for Dr. Ray's service to her for as she says, "Dr. Ray saved my life." She

85

also remembers Oly as part of that "lifesaving" time as one who also helped to heal her.

Oly was 17 years old when she died and her body had become a burden to her throughout the last year. However, as we sat in the vet's awaiting our appointment for her euthanasia, a young boy excitedly told his mother to see the pretty kitten . . . indeed she had a radiant glow to her through her most difficult of times. She always loved the hands-on and Attunements that I shared with her every day of her life with me. In addition, I had the joy to have a network of radiant humans to support my hands and my heart as I held her in her last few moments of life in her small cat body.

I had a gentle vet who insists that the animal receive a painless exit, not a jolting death shot. I had asked Dr. Ray and a circle of radiant friends to network with us as we went through the process. We were both so fortunate to be receiving a bombardment of radiant support—that even this woman veterinarian was surprised at how well things went. I spent the last few moments before we went into the room in much the same way that I had spent the last few days of her life—enjoying watching her play (a bit slowly but with curiosity still intact), having her curl up with hands-on and feeling and experiencing that wonderful purr. I was moving the Cosmic Symbols through the various parts of her body as I held her, and I created the Attunements with her, embracing her with healing and sustaining energy. I did cry as we held one another, Oly and I, for I really knew a deep sorrow in realizing that I would miss her very special cat personality in my life. She continued to purr.

She even purred when the vet gave her the first shot to let her drift to sleep; it was so painless she was totally comfortable. She was peaceful and trusting in her last moments and I felt the releasing of the life force within her as a very natural letting go. She was there one moment and then, although her loving energy field was still in my heart, she was gone. Her life as a cat named Oly was over and she was a very warm, and soft, and loving energy filling the room. I remained alone with her form for a little while adjusting to her new "form" of being, and creating the Attunements. All I can say in these words is that her new way of being is light, full of moving, and seems so very much larger than before. Sensing her in those moments was like feeling the wind—present and embracing yet not tangible in the ordinary sense. Experiencing her is and was in those moments very inspiring. Experiencing with her that great release is a moment that is alive for me.

It was also a real celebration! She was released from a body that had become painful and arthritic. She had been trapped in much too small a vehicle for her as she lived those last months. Her great heart and love were much larger and more encompassing than the tiny body she lived in. Radiantly, she lives on with me in my heart as a glorious remembering of our times of gentle companionship, love and joy. A cat 17 years old that still chased her tail for, indeed, each day was the *first time* she ever saw it. Oh, what she taught me in our time together! She knew this universal and radiant energy without a hesitation. She came immediately to wherever hands-on or Attunements were being done; she followed the radiant energy and appeared–instantly! What she taught me could make a book in itself. What a server she was and is to this day in my life and many others!

Several of the radiant friends who were part of that warm and healing network of energy that I experienced with her leaving grew from their opportunity to participate in her death. Following is one of their sharings:

"Lady Olympia was my first cat. Up until her, I had always been a dog person. So, she introduced me to the warmth, attention and nurturing ways that a cat can bring into a human's life.

"As she grew older, she continued to evolve in personality and mannerisms. She was a fine model for aging because she didn't stop changing and being new each day. Yes, she became slower in her movements and less active in her play, but she never stopped interacting with me and with others.

"I was with some other alumni of TRT when Oly was making her transition. Since we had been alerted to the time of the process, we each chose to work with her exit from these outer planes with various tools of The Radiance Technique.

"I chose to do The Polarity Exercise as explained in *The Official Handbook of The Radiance Technique.*® I placed both hands on my Heart Center.

"I put Oly and my love for her under my right hand, and I imaged a counter-clockwise spiral moving through my right hand and through Oly and her love and nurturing energies and my heart.

"Under my left hand I imaged my emotional body response to Oly's leaving—my emotions of sadness and regret and loss for not having her to play with and pet in the moments and hours and days to come. And I imaged another counter-clockwise spiral moving through my left hand and through Oly's energy as I *felt* her in my emotional body and through my heart.

"After a few moments, I imaged the counter-clockwise spiral moving through both hands and through my heart, continuously, non-stop.

"And in that energy, I felt my release of Oly. I sensed, I *knew* in that spiraling energy something greater than Oly in her outer planes and me in mine—that under one hand I still imaged her outer form . . . yet, under the other, and through my heart, I sensed her expansion into something infinite in scope.

"I sensed the energy of her release not just from her earthbound pains and aging but from the confines of her earth-bound body and outer planes. I sensed that this cycle of leaving for her was a release—a freedom!—to unlimited existence.

"And, I realized then that I was no longer sad about her leaving."

Fred. W. Wright, Jr,
The Fourth Degree
Florida

As each of these sharings tell us, every animal gives to us so much more than we expect for they are unconditional in their relationship toward us. The sadness we feel when they leave our lives is tempered with the joy of their release. The techniques for using TRT suggested by these alumni are supports for you. They can support your participation in the death and dying process more aware of the energies at work. Many people have chosen to go through the process rather than avoid it with their animal friend when they have not yet done so with a human friend. And, as they have shared, a great time of expansion and growth is beyond that door of participation, a deep time of sharing with an animal companion made more natural and joyous while using TRT.

SUPPORTING YOURSELF WITH RADIANT ENERGY

You may need to look more deeply into your own feelings following the death of a beloved animal companion. There are a range of emotional responses which are very normal. After all, your life changes and your daily interactions are different from that moment on in the realm of the outer planes of the physical, emotional and mental dynamic of your life energy. And, other animals in the household will be feeling the differences as well. You may want to use TRT more extensively with them as a hands-on process or if you have studied to The Second Degree and beyond, directing energy to animal(s) at home when you are away at work, or attuning with the animal that is missing its friend. Animals, however, can sometimes move through these changes and cycles in life more naturally than humans. I invite you to remember your own process and support yourself with TRT.

Many animal caretakers experience their sense of loss in very intense ways. We would like to offer some suggestions for moving through these feelings to grow with them rather than to suppress or ignore them.

Anger: As you experience this feeling, you are probably trying to assign "blame" for what has occurred. Our cultural upbringing tells us that for every event there is a cause. Then, for things we don't like, that cause is to "blame" for the situation. Equally on the opposite side of this polarity is the idea that for the things that happen that you do like, something or someone should receive the "credit" for the situation.

First, you may be angry with yourself for allowing the situation to occur or for contributing in some way through your neglect to the death of your animal friend. You may also blame the vet for not taking the proper actions or for not finding the "cure" for the sick or injured animal. Normally, you would be able to move through these feelings–but, here the loss is permanent and felt deeply. Your hands-on for yourself can be the most valuable tool for growth you have ever used during these times. In her section on "Anger" in *The Expanded Reference Manual*, Dr. Ray suggests that when you are "experiencing anger, use immediately right-at-the-time Front Position #1 and/or in combination Front Positions #1 and #3. Then, balance your energies by using Head Positions #2, #3 and #4 or any combinations therein and Back Position #3. Even just a few minutes in these positions will be supportive to you!"

Guilt: This feeling is closely related to the anger you may turn on yourself since that is what guilt actually is . . . anger at yourself for something you did wrong or didn't do right to help the animal you took responsibility for. This sense of shame and guilt can be devastating if you are unaware of how it is robbing you of your growth. Sometimes there may even be some facts that support your guilty feelings. However, you need to use TRT hands-on daily to let yourself see the whole picture of your relationship and responsibility. It is a real growth to be able to take responsibility for your actions or inactions and still not stop yourself from moving on through guilt. Guilt often provides a way to distract yourself from moving through and learning from the experience at hand. The whole hands-on session is very necessary for interacting with strong guilt feelings and especially using Front Position #1 in various combinations such as Front #2, #3, and Back #3 to open your heart to loving yourself and learning to release yourself from guilt.

Depression: Dr. Ray suggests in her entry on this subject in *The Expanded Reference Manual* that you "apply the complete session for energy balancing and harmonizing on a daily basis with extended use of Head Positions #2 and #3, Front #1 and #3 and Back #1, #2 and #3. It is important to remember to make a conscious choice to use TRT when you are actually experiencing and aware of your sense of depression."

"Grief" or the grieving process are opportunities for transformation. In *The Expanded Reference Manual*, Dr. Ray has written positively of these opportunities: "The deep sadness that can be felt at a time of loss is one that each individual participates with in different ways. TRT can be used to access whole energy that is supportive to a natural unfolding of the feelings that can accompany the grieving process. Spending time daily to apply the entire hands-on session gives you the opportunity to be with yourself and explore your feelings, releasing them in ways that are safe and harmless to yourself. During the hands-on session, explore spending time in particular positions that support your explorations. You may wish to spend extended time with all four Head Positions, Front Positions #1 and/or #3, and/or Back Position #3 affirming the universal cycles of birth and death that are part of all *living* experiences."

The grief process itself is not on a time table. You may move through some feelings, think they are gone only to have them recur in a moment of grief and missing of your friend. Immediately use your hands-on to be in touch with your own deeper realizations and your own capacity to grow through your sorrowful feelings. As all of the sharings in this chapter suggest, individual experiences are different and unique. Yet, there is a common thread of conscious choice in these sharings. Every one of them has had a realization of expansion and growth, a deepening of their heart, through their use of The Radiance Technique. TRT offers you loving support for your journey and awareness of the significance of a time of transition in the cycles of the life process.

Animals and plants are an integral part of our planetary system, and their destiny is linked with ours.

Barbara Ray, Ph.D.

Love is the master of everything we do.

John Denver, One World Album

CHAPTER SEVEN

COMMUNICATION BEYOND THE OUTER PLANES

The greatest laboratory for gathering experiential data on our interactions with radiant energy and animals is life itself. Events in our lives and in the world offer daily opportunities to share The Radiance Technique® with individual animals and with corresponding members of a particular species. Dr. Barbara Ray has written movingly about animals in all of her books, and in her classes she has encouraged students to move beyond the visible outer form of relationships with animals to communicate with them in many ways. Many students of TRT have discovered a deepening awareness of the inner planes as they have shared radiant energy with animals and often their sense of the global or planetary relationships between humans and animals becomes even clearer.

The Radiance Technique® is an inner planes science, beginning with The First Degree, for the hands-on session itself is a inner-connection with radiant, universal energy–*beyond* the level of touch. For every student there is the possibility of using hands-on both with and without touch as a tool for communication and gentle relating and educating. The hands-on can be applied at a level of 1 to 2 inches above the level of the skin so that animals in severe pain or who have just had surgery can be supported by the hands-on process beyond the level of touch. This application can be used by every student of TRT from The First Degree onward. You can use this method of hands-on to go beyond the visible outer planes and you can do this when there is no crisis or need, as a form of deepening the bonds and communication with one another.

For example, you can use your hands over the sleeping animal to generate a universal energy uniting with the animal's energy field, harmlessly and with no intrusion. You can use your hands with and without touch as you play together, walk together, rest together. Most animals are active and restive in different cycles than the human and using hands-on without touch can assist you to share with your animal friends no matter what their cycle of the moment.

For every student who has studied to The Second Degree and beyond, specific methods are taught for precise ways to direct radiant, universal energy. In using these inner planes "hands-on" methods, you can broaden and deepen your outreach with animals everywhere, interacting with endangered species in locations far from your home. The inner planes exist beyond the dimensions of the outer planes of the physical, emotional and mental planes of energy. Dr. Ray has called these "the more lasting bodies" that we have. Using TRT you may reach beyond the limits of time and space for your interactions with animals. Friends around the world interact in this way with their sharing of universal, light-energy of The Radiance Technique® for their animal friends. In other chapters there are further suggestions for additional support through the Cosmic Symbols and the directing of energy, and the use of the Attunement Processes to deepen the inner planes communication between humans and animals.

Many students have written to us about their experiences with animals who live with them and that these experiences seem "telepathic" in that often no verbal words are exchanged. They are describing the deeper inner dimensions that they have discovered that goes beyond words and actually beyond the physical, emotional or mental level of communication. Most people who have used TRT tell us that their animal friends just "know" when they are doing hands-on or directing energy or doing Attunements. The animal just appears as the Attunements are being done.

RADIANT INTERACTIONS AROUND THE GLOBE

The communication that takes place between human and animal beyond touch and beyond mind happens in vastly different locations. Animals that are in the "wild" also communicate with and respond to the person sharing radiant energy with them. The depths of the sea are comfortable surroundings for this student who shares his discovery adventure:

"The joys of The Radiance Technique are still new to me even today, but this summer was a wonder all its own. Bermuda being a small island in the sub-tropics, we enjoy a broad variety of water sports. One of these is scuba diving.

"I am an avid diver and I have been certified since I was fifteen; this summer, however, was a new experience altogether. This summer, I was a diver who possessed The Radiant Second Degree, and extending my dive time was only one of the benefits I was to experience while diving.

"My diving buddy was a seafood lover so it was only natural that while diving he looked for lobster and large fish so that he could dream about dinner. I forbad him to do anything but look and dream, and that suited him fine. When he finds a lobster cave, he likes to lie on the bottom and tickle their whips, if they are brave enough to venture out. I have always just looked over his shoulder; this summer I decided to try it myself to see if my radiant hands made any difference.

"We found a cave and I motioned that I wished to try this time alone, so he backed off and watched while I stretched out one hand and offered it to the occupants of the cave. Slowly at first and then quicker, as they gained confidence in my immobility and my partner's distance, all of the lobsters crowded forward to investigate my outstretched hand. There were twelve altogether of various sizes, and after a brush from each of them they seemed to back up for a conference between themselves while I risked a glance at my partner. He was as intrigued as I was and signed to continue my experiment.

"When I looked back in the direction of the cave, I was lost in wonder at what I saw. They seemed to have made a decision amongst themselves and were waiting for me to do something about it. While diving I wear gloves to protect my hands from the coral and other nasties that you find on a reef. During my experiment I had kept it on to protect my hand from the lobsters' spines. Lobsters don't have claws as they are really crayfish, but they have sharp spines which point forward all over their whips and heads. I got a very strong impression that I was being asked by them to trust them and remove my glove.

"I pulled my hand back and took my glove off, keeping my movements slow and even, and let my now bare hand lie palm up on the sand before them. To my amazement one by one they took a turn standing on my hand. They lifted their larger pair of whips high above their own heads careful not to harm my hand as they crawled on and off of it. The last lobster was the oldest and largest in the cave and when she stood over my hand she paused and looked me right in the eye as she lowered her whips gently to touch my face mask. She was the largest lobster I haver ever seen, with legs as thick as two of my fingers side by side. She was gorgeous, magnificent. I could feel the energy flowing through my hand into her, and then back flavored with her spirit. Just for a moment I forgot I was human and had to return to the hectic pace of the world of men. Just for a moment all I was, was a quiet peace; feeling the currents of the reef as they brushed over and around me.

"I must have twitched or perhaps my partner moved in too close; either way the spell was broken as she backed quickly away and back to the safety of her cave, and if lobsters could frown, I'm sure she was frowning at some thought or other.

"After that dive my friend asked me how I had done that. He was so moved by what he saw that he has sworn off eating lobster from now on, and he encourages me to 'experiment' anytime we go diving together.

"During another dive with him, I used my Second Degree techniques to direct energy to both of us during the time we were underwater. I have always used less air than he, and during this particular dive, not only were our breathing and heart rates entrained but we got an extra half-hour's worth of air out of our tanks. What should have been a one-hour dive was a one-and-a-half-hour dive, and the fish we encountered loved us.

"We would swim into schools of reef fish, and they would follow us around the reef, brushing me as they went by and eyeing my partner as well. Although they came close to him, they did not seem to want to touch him that often.

"If I let my hands hang down or held them out in front of me, the fish would press their sides into my palms as they swam by.

"One large Amber Jack who was in the area left his school to follow my partner and I through a cave system under the reef we were exploring that day. When we emerged on the other side we found ourselves in an undersea labyrinth made up of canyons twisting in and out of coral castles which stood above shell holes arrayed like galleons at their feet.

"With so many places to explore and each seeing something different to catch our eyes, my partner and I got briefly separated in the maze. Not at all concerned over this occurrence, I swam over to investigate some star coral which had grown in the shape of a natural stair case ascending from the grotto floor to the coral above. A tugging on one of my straps got my attention, so I turned around to see the Jack impatiently waiting for me to notice him.

"I offered him a shrug to show that I did not know what it was he wanted from me. As my shoulders came down, he swam up to my right hand and pushed at it with his head. He had me curious no so I turned my hand over to see what he wanted with it. As soon as my palm was turned up, he swam onto it and stopped. His belly was swollen where it touched my hand and he seemed to be trying to stay in position against the current which was washing over us.

"He let me close my hand enough to support him and hold him still. As I knelt on the sandy bottom with the Amber Jack in my hand, my diving partner swam by the mouth of the grotto searching for me. I did not want to move and disturb the fish so I just tracked his exhaust bubbles as he searched a neighboring shell hole. After a few minutes had passed, my agitation began to grow and must have been communicated to the Jack as he turned an eye to look at me. My agitation disappeared and I relaxed once more, noticing as I did that the swelling was smaller than it had been when we had started this strange exchange.

"Soon after, the Jack swam lazily out of my hand and circled me once before swimming off in a straight line over the reef. He kept pausing and dodging back toward me asking me to follow him. He led me straight to my partner who was surprised to see me following a fish over the reef top toward him. The fish circled us both and then swam away on his own.

"So, next time you are out in the wilds, be it on the land or the sea, be sure to share this loving energy with your surroundings, too. After all, it is universal! Who knows what adventure awaits you, what lesson to be learned from a furry or fish friend!"

T. Bruce Chapman
The Third Degree (3A)
Bermuda

Beginning to direct energy beyond any physical or time or space boundaries can be exhilarating and deeply moving. You actually become aware of another living energy beyond your own mind's capacity to understand. An Australian student had a very unpredictable experience that happened from the directing itself and not from her thoughts about the possibilities. She offers us this sharing:

"In 1986, I studied The First Degree. Twelve months later I studied The Second Degree Program. This was a new concept for me. I had always believed that healing at a distance was possible but to create the Cosmic Symbols, direct the radiant energy and to know for a fact that the connections were made is another thing.

"During the time, I lived in a large house about 300-350 feet from the Murray River. Along the banks were magnificent stands of River Red Guras 80-100 feet high, large old trees that an abundance of bird life had made their home. For several months before I received The Second Degree, an owl had taken up residence in a tree nearby. This owl started screeching at dusk and continued non-stop until dawn. (Owls are fairly silent birds and this behavior was completely out of character). This screeching kept going on night after night, not letting me sleep. I would wander down to the river during the night and pinpoint my noisy friend by torchlight. The bird would sit and watch me, even on the lower branches.

"Lying in bed at 2 or 3 a.m. one night (I was unable to sleep), I empathized with this owl, feeling all was not well. I strongly visualized the owl and proceeded to direct it the healing energy of The Radiance Technique. The

INSTANT I connected with the four head positions, the owl stopped screeching. This startled me and I began again to direct energy again. Again, a connection instantly stopped the screeching. The same reaction happened when I directed the radiant energy to the four front positions. It started screeching when I moved to the four back positions.

"I continued directing to the owl for most of the winter with similar reactions, the screeching finishing as winter left. To have a positive, undeniable and loud . . . as well as unplanned proof of the radiant power and practice was wonderful. Undreamed of visual, aural and emotional proof that the beautiful energy is alive and well, no matter what, who or where you are!"

Helen Strickland
The Second Degree
Australia

Discoveries abound when you use radiant energy with different animal species. Here is a sharing from South America:

"I was recently on holiday with my family in the Galapagos Islands of Ecuador. One day, a female seal fleeing from a male came and sat right next to me! My companions held their breaths, because the other seals were really furious. I was also a little afraid because of the size of the seals, but I remembered to use my Second Degree techniques. After that, the male went off by himself and the female became calm again."

Elizabeth Bez
The Second Degree
Venezuela

So many people learn to trust more and to interact differently when they use radiant energy with animals. This student discovered something about herself and a very different animal when she met a Florida manatee for the first time:

"In the early morning, I started jogging. I asked to be led to an interesting place. Then, I saw the ocean! I ran fast, delighted about all the big pelicans swimming and floating around. Suddenly, I noticed a sign, telling something about manatees. I walked down to the water: nothing. Then, I saw them: a big fish—perhaps a shark. Then some big noses. I identified one mother with a baby and one single manatee. Slowly I undressed and entered the water, swam around. Nothing to be seen. Did I chase them away? I was about to leave the water, when I saw 'him.' Close to me, he was floating around, his tail pointing towards me. I shared an Attunement with this sweet, ancient-looking creature, related with the elephants. He turned around, coming nearer, so that I could even touch him!

"He was attracted to me, i.e. the light energy I was pouring into him. In this deep light connection, we stayed for minutes, time became eternity. 'Oh, great center who relates us all' came popping up from my heart. (A line from an ancient Power Chant–see "Reflections," page 118). Two totally harmless beings meeting and touching each other's heart, becoming an example of how relationships among all living beings are meant to be.

"When I slowly walked back to the beach, the manatee turned around, his big arms pointing out of the water, moving slowly, as if waving goodbye. In the distance, I saw the mother and her calf. It was as if time stood still. It came to my mind: 'How do you enjoy your *Being*?' instead of 'How do you *do*?'

Barbara Simonsohn
The Fourth Degree
Germany

In the following sharing, you have a sense of joy and participation that comes from this student's capacity to direct radiant, supportive, universal energy.

"After receiving The Second Degree in The Radiance Technique,® I immediately incorporated The Second Degree Techniques and cosmic symbols in my work and energy exchanges with animals. Whenever possible or practical, I still apply hands-on with the animals; however, with The Second Degree tools for directing energy and the Cosmic Symbols, I work more on the inner planes with the animals. The majority of my energy exchanges and interactions with animals occur on the interior. In addition, whenever possible or practical, I also regularly pattern the symbols on the animals' heads and share heart melds with the animals.

"First, one of the most profoundly soothing and kind applications of The Second Degree for me is to be able to immediately direct energy and pattern the symbols to an animal whenever I see that one has been hurt or killed on the highway. Without The Radiance Technique® and the tools I can use, I would feel badly for the poor creature and feel helpless. Now, I still am sorry that the creature met with tragedy and has made its transition, but I am able to immediately respond. I am able to 'do something' I can support the animal and direct energy to it on the inner planes.

"When I respond to such situations with my Second Degree tools and symbols, two experiences occur for me. Mentally, I am able to remain centered and balanced. I am aware of the inevitable cycle of nature and I am more consciously aware of change, evolution, transitions and transformation. Mentally, I know that I can help support the animal at that moment in the Here Now which transcends normal time frames. And, emotionally, my heart does not hurt as much. I feel a lessening of an overly emotional response that is a negative experience for me and a waste of my emotional energies. Emotionally, I am able to remain centered and balanced."

JoJean Ewart, Ph.D.
The Radiant Third Degree
Washington

Using her capacity for directing energy and attunements, a student of TRT expanded her sense of deep communication when she wrote the following:

"While on a photo safari in Kenya at the Masai Mara Wild Game Reserve, I was deeply moved and honored to be in this expansive territory where so many wild animals live freely and harmoniously. I experienced herds of wildebeest migrating with zebras as well as giraffes, impalas, gazelles, topi, wart hogs, hyenas, elephants, lions, baboons, hippos and crocodiles, *all living in balance.*

"We traveled in a land cruiser through the reserve and I had many opportunities to direct this radiant energy as well as take photos. I was also talking to the animals, sharing my joy with them. The animals seemed to hear me; the giraffes were posing, the hippos smiled, and my colleagues said that they had never experienced anyone who could communicate with the animals as I was doing. They commented more than once as these radiant beings responded to what we all share–Radiance!

"I also experienced the Masai tribe people who lived on their land by herding their goats and cattle along with the wild animals. As I directed radiant energy we shared 'eye to eye', 'smile to smile' and 'heart to heart.' Throughout this entire journey with Radiance sharing, I now have a deeper awareness that We All Are Truly One! Shanti!"

Mary Lou Dains
The Fourth Degree
Arizona

DEEPENING THE INNER COMMUNICATION

The profound relationship between human and animal that can be established using The Radiance Technique® is only now being talked about and written about as students take a more consistent approach to the communication they have with animals and observe the relationship that develops. A student of TRT shares a natural development of her work with the High Noon Peace Network and her sharing with animals:

"Last month I stayed at a friend's apartment while she was away and shared it with her cat. At noon on the first full day that I was there, I sat in the living room reading when the cat jumped into my lap and I was reminded of the time (High Noon). Using the Cosmic Symbols I have learned, I let the cat represent the planet earth and all its living beings and I Attuned all of us as part of the High Noon Peace Networking. Then I sat with my hands on my new cat friend for thirty minutes directing energy to the planet from the inner planes.

"The cat lay very still and soft in my lap. I closed my eyes and together we joined the Whole of Existence in its inner nature. I was an experience out of time and space and a deeply loving one. It was clear to me that we had entered another dimension while we simultaneously sat on a living room sofa and that we had done it together. As I write of it now, I am certain I know what 'bonding' means and that the tool we have, as alumni of The Radiance

101

Technique®, is a powerful means for bonding with nature in all her shapes and forms."

Katherine Lenel
The Fourth Degree
Florida

Even people who do not yet have The Radiance Technique® have written a number of books and articles that describe experiences of "of exceptional degrees of communication between humans and animals." In the book, "Kinship with All Life," J. Allen Boone describes how he established a form of telepathic rapport with the German Shepherd dog, Strongheart."

SERVING ANIMALS

Boone wrote, too, of "the distinction between training an animal and educating one. In his view training an animal was relatively easy and placed emphasis on the physical level and upon the authority of the trainer. . . . (In educating an animal) the animal is treated as an intelligent fellow being and the educator works with intelligence, integrity and imagination to help make use of its thinking faculties and so develop character."

For those who have studied The Radiance Technique, the process of training and working with animals of all kinds has practical aspects as well as in this sharing from England:

"I also use TRT on animals. My husband rears calves for herd replacement and TRT is invaluable for getting them to drink from a bucket. This process normally takes about a week. When I use the hands-on radiant energy, I can get them drinking on their own from a bucket in less than one day. TRT is also good for their general growth and well-being and calmness."

Iris Houghton
The Second Degree
England

Your use of The Radiance Technique® and its inner communication through universal energy provides you with a global tool that is helping to build a bridge of healing and wholeness between humans and animals.

This student discovered a profound inner-connection with the principle of expansion while attuning an endangered species:

"During a free-lance journalism assignment a few years ago, I was able to see and be with for more than an hour the last of four surviving members of a vanishing species. I was at a small, out-of-the-way corner of Walt Disney World in Orlando, Fla., out of sight of the tens of thousands of tourists who visit this massive theme park each year.

"The park was the protected home for the last four Dusky Seaside Sparrows on the planet. They were all male. The species used to live in the tall grasses and marshes of the area around Orlando that had long since been developed into communities and tourist attractions. All efforts to find more Dusky Seaside Sparrows–and especially female ones–had failed.

"While at the park to interview the Sparrows' caretaker, I was able to spend a long stretch of time outside their cages, just watching the sparrows hop and feed in their cages. And I was also able to attune each one to The First and The Second Degree levels of The Radiance Technique,® so that they could continue their process of extinction with the expansion of these attunement processes.

"The last male Dusky Seaside Sparrow died last year. Mixed with my sadness that yet another species was now gone forever from this planet was the lesson I had learned while attuning these sparrows–that all of us can experience expansion while we are here on the planet, and we can carry that expansion into whatever the next stage of evolution is for each of us.

Fred. W. Wright Jr.
The Fourth Degree
Florida

Whether you are interacting with an animal that lives with you or an animal that is endangered and far away from you, we encourage you to place a priority in your relationships with animals to work with education as well as communication, creatively expanding the intelligence and knowledge of all animals with whom you come in contact. To do so is to be guided by the natural relationship that animals have with humans, rather than imposing human values upon them.

Animals in our homes can often be over-analyzed. They do not compete for attention, for instance, as humans do. They are much more natural. They just want the attention for themselves, not to keep it from another. Jealousy is a human reaction, a feeling of loss of attention, a psychological behavior. Animals simply are right in the present tense, discovering in the moment. The attention they want can be in any form—petting, hands-on, or some form of playing (which with them is always a discovery process). If you've observed and experienced young animals, they don't wait for an appropriate time for play, or time for touch, or time for discovery. That's a human concept. Their sense of time is right now!

Touch, or play, or discovery are natural to them, not pre-planned, pre-evaluated behaviors. It is our responsibility to realize that they do NOT naturally have our psychological habits. Too often, we do not just observe what they want or how they are interacting, especially if they are living with us instead of playing naturally in the fields or open spaces on earth. We put a value judgment or projection of ourselves and then label their actions with our opinions. As we use The Radiance Technique® in our relationships, we can learn a great deal about naturalness and being in the present and of participating in discovery from the animals who live with us.

COMPANIONSHIP AND SERVICE: A TRUE GIFT OF UNCONDITIONAL LOVE

There is so much to discover about the animal and its communication with us! Their forms of communication, such as purring, barking, chirping, whinnying, or cuddling and nuzzling, have most often been thought of as expressions of their companionship with us. Animals that live domestically with humans are very unconditional companions. They naturally respond to us no matter what our "mood" is. This unconditional animal response to the human friend is what draws many humans to adopt an animal friend to live with them. However, there is so much more for us to know of their gifts to us.

Diana Reiss, a researcher who studies communications among captive dolphins, thinks that "there may be something fully analogous to human language in the behavior of animals—a something that's not even vocal."

A student who was in Canada singing in the Opera shares meeting two dolphins in the Edmonton Mall:

"I went into the interior section of their pool . . . and knelt on the edge and began feeding them the fish that the trainer had given me. When the feeding was over (all the while I was offering them the energy of TRT as well as the fishes), I stayed there, beckoning them to my Radiant Touch. Much to my surprise and delight, they continued to come to my hands—fully aware that I was no longer feeding them—and presented me with the crowns of their heads; THEN they began to do a shimmying dance from the bottom of the pool and would come up out of the water on their tails so that I could reach their Heart Centers. They kept coming again and again in their 'tail walk' for more radiant touching! What joy for all of us! An incredible experience in loving communications and one-ness with another wondrous and unique life form here on Planet Earth!"

Clarity James
The Fourth Degree
Virginia

A striking example of this non-vocal "communication," was chronicled in January, 1992 on a television news program. A research site in Florida called Dolphins Plus in Key Largo, has a swim therapy program in which properly trained helpers are involved with children who are physically or mentally impaired. The children become deeply relaxed while swimming with these animal helpers, and they frequently begin a process of recovery and stability. However, the most dramatic example of the dolphins as helpers for their human charges was one concerning a little boy suffering from congenital heart disease who had undergone three open heart surgeries, had paralysis and partial blindness and been in an 8-day coma. He refused to cooperate with his own recovery process; he did not trust humans any longer. He had suffered considerable pain. When he went into the program the 40-pound child was paired with a 700-pound dolphin named Fonzi. Remarkably, Fonzi not only carefully began to manipulate the weakened little boy to move in the water, pushing and supporting him where his fragile limbs could not move, but he began to "play" with the boy in ways that required the child to rebuild the necessary muscle skills for play. For instance, Fonzi tossed and tossed and tossed a ball to the boy to get him to move arms and hands that could not–at that time–toss a ball. Gentle and compassionate, the dolphin has been the guide for the recovery of this boy who 8 months after he began the program could carry a bucket of fish to feed his friend, when only months before he couldn't even move his hand. Doctors had said he would never sing, never walk, never run. Fonzi has helped him to gradually move and walk and run, communicating with him and sharing "play" and support throughout his recovery. The boy's mother feels that their bond, an obvious inner communication, is so strong that neither will ever forget it. She expresses a profound gratitude for the experience her son has shared as he continues his recovery process.

Researchers at Dolphins Plus, where the dolphins are not retained but are willing volunteers, believe that these compassionate beings may even "know when they don't know something," opening the possibility that they may be "self-aware." In the animal kingdom, prior to this ongoing research, only humans were known to have the capacity for self-awareness.

In *The Expanded Reference Manual*, which is quoted with permission, Dr. Ray states that Self-Awareness "refers to a state of being aware of the dynamics of your ego and your beingness as a Self in Existence with a Life process." And she has supported us that "(it) is a power which can be developed and expanded. Self-awareness has to do with awakeness and consciously directing your attention. Without developing your powers of self-awareness there can be no awakening to your inner reality, to your inner dimensions of soul and spirit. TRT is a cosmic science of universal energy giving direct access to the inner dynamic. Using TRT on a regular basis and participating in your ongoing, expanding, transforming process supports and enhances the expansion of your self-awareness." We can use TRT, especially as Dr. Ray suggests–"Head Positions #1 and #3, and Front Position #1 for extended times in mediation" on a daily basis to further develop self-awareness beyond the narrow confines of our knowledge of ourselves psychologically or physically. As part of my own daily program of using TRT as Dr. Ray has suggested, I have added a daily remembering that as a human I have the *power* of self-awareness. As I am doing my hands-on in the morning, I keep making a choice to be more aware. It is so easy to drift into aimless thinking, moving in my

106

mind to the past or the future and losing the impact of this very moment. During the day, I often now do remember that "I have the power of self-awareness". This is a vital support for me in my growth process as I reach to use my mental plane to find an "answer" to something which actually requires the self-aware observer of me to respond. It is also a great help to repeat this affirmation when I sink into an emotional response without awareness. A quick remembering, accompanied especially for me with Front Position #1, that "I have the *power* of self-awareness" can bring me more in contact with my Real Self and not my psychological self or its limitations. I keep remembering that the dolphin who helped the child was absolutely in the moment with the boy and not "wasting" any energy with aimlessness. It was focused in the Here Now and doing naturally an interaction of support. What an inspiration for my own expansion of self-awareness!

ANIMALS SHARING LOVING SERVICE WITH HUMANS

The expansion of service with animals helping humans has grown in the last few years as humans realize the wonderful resource that animals are. Increasing use of domesticated animals to help the blind, the elderly, the handicapped and those in hospitals and other institutions has proved useful in developing human understanding of animal "language" and of receiving the unconditional gifts of loving that animals bring to humans. They are silent servers in ways we may never fully discover.

Throughout the world there are now programs, such as Riding Therapy for the Disabled and Guide Dogs for the Blind, where animals provide needed companionship, skill and support, gifts that improve the quality of life of the people who come in contact with them.

Many creative initiatives are being pioneered in this field. As an example, The Guide Dog Association of New South Wales, Australia, started its Pets as Therapy Programme in 1978. Since then over 1,000 dogs have been placed in hospitals, nursing homes, homes for the mentally handicapped and with disabled people. Such animals help reduce the negative effects of institutional life and their presence has been found to be of enormous benefit to both patients and staff.

In addition, in the United States and in Canada, many children who are considered differently abled benefit from

107

"Riding Therapy," a specific approach to using horseback riding as a therapeutic support. One student who has studied to The Third Degree of TRT works with this program in Canada and first brought it to our attention.

Through their natural energy of harmlessness and service animals affect humans deeply. Television entertainer and animal supporter Betty White recently recounted on TV a dramatic story of a young boy who was placed, leg braces and all, on a Riding Therapy trained horse for the first time. He had been unable to walk unassisted. The Riding Therapy experience was so profound and exciting for him that when he was lifted off the horse, and not placed immediately back in his wheelchair, he at first simply stood upright and then he moved to take three steps toward the immobile horse to pat him in gratitude. Those were his first steps unassisted! An animal had touched him so deeply that he moved to give his appreciation and overcame a physical barrier!

Animals have also been part of programs that offer support for the elderly with a cat or a dog making all the difference in the lovingness and alertness of the older person. Cats have also been instrumental in "bringing out" autistic children as they petted and held the cats. These children are often considered "unreachable" for communication. A regular program in the midwest called "Paws with a Cause" is part of the United Way efforts in its community.

In all of these kinds of projects animals are chosen for their calming and loving attributes. The horses, cats or dogs undergo training for the job and are screened carefully for the correct overall disposition. However, the biggest asset they bring to their efforts in these programs is their natural, unconditional and loving response to the humans they "work" with. Their natural service to humankind is unlike any learning process that humans must go through. What a joy to add The Radiance Technique to the lives of these selfless beings. It is our opportunity to serve those who already serve us in the unseen ways of their heartfelt support.

Many people who work with animals in these ways remark upon the animals' sense of "responsibility". Those who have TRT and have shared their animals in such service programs tell us that their own learning is deeply enhanced by this process. The energy of responsibility is certainly coming from an expanded animal, giving of itself to the human family. Researchers discovered over 15 years ago that dolphins, for instance, exhibit altruistic behavior. That sense of responsibility and service can be expanded upon by each of us as we honor with hands-on, the directing of radiant energy, and sharing attunements with animals wherever we meet them, on the outer planes or through the dimensions of the inner planes.

Reader's Note: Research for this chapter has come from many sources. However, the World Goodwill Newsletter, a quarterly bulletin printed in 1990 by the Lucis Trust, entitled "Animal Rights, Expanding the Circle of Ethics and Compassion," from which some of the data was reprinted will provide interested readers with more details on that subject. With the help of this bulletin, a listing of resources for co-operating organizations in many countries is printed in Chapter 8 "Resources Worldwide." Please also see the Selected Bibliography for further information on book references.

Animals and plants exhibit an awareness different from ours, yet they share with us intelligence, natural growth cycles, health, disease, and death. Different does not mean inferior!
Barbara Ray, Ph.D.

CHAPTER EIGHT

RESOURCES WORLDWIDE

One of my primary resources is The Radiance Technique Association International, Inc. (T.R.T.A.I.), P.O. Box 40570, St. Petersburg, Florida, 33743-0570, a nonprofit organization which is a membership organization and provides information for those who wish to know more about TRT. The T.R.T.A.I. publishes several issues per year of *The Radiance Technique Journal*, which includes an ongoing column in each issue dedicated to the sharings of using TRT with animals. From its resources came some of the sharings for this book. Additionally, radiant animal friends responded to an ad in the *Journal*, sending their experiences and permission to use them.

I would like to express my deepest gratitude to all of the many radiant friends and alumni of TRT who have shared their experiences to make this book possible. I would particularly like to express my appreciation to Crystal Sierra who researched many of the individual sharings in the files from the many years of producing *The Radiance Technique Journal*; and to Fred. W. Wright, Jr. who searched the archives for the original sharings and any follow-up or additions to them, as well as other material from T.R.T.A.I. and the *Journal*.

In this chapter I would also like to extend to you some resources developed while researching this book. These resources are cooperating organizations around the globe who have the support of animals or wildlife or specific species as their interest. The list is by no means complete but may serve as a beginning for your own interests and inner or outer levels of support.

One of the inspiring resources used in this book is the Suncoast Seabird Sanctuary. Here is some additional information about that organization:

Suncoast Seabird Sanctuary, Inc.

The Suncoast Seabird Sanctuary, Inc. was founded in 1971 by zoologist Ralph T. Heath, Jr. The Sanctuary is the largest wild bird hospital in the U.S. and is dedicated to the rescue, repair, recuperation and release of sick and injured wild birds. A non-profit organization, the Sanctuary operates entirely on tax deductible donations from the general public. The Suncoast Seabird Sanctuary started unofficially on December 3, 1971 when Ralph found a Cormorant walking along an boulevard on the Gulf Beaches, dragging a broken wing. He took it to a St. Petersburg veterinarian who operated on it and gave it back to Ralph for its recuperation. As word spread, other injured seabirds began to arrive at Ralph's backyard.

Although the original Cormorant ("Maynard") recovered fully from his wounds, he would never fly again. Since Ralph would have to keep him, it was necessary to obtain a permit to keep a wild bird in captivity. The beginning of the Sanctuary was as simple as that.

The Sanctuary is proud to have treated, rehabilitated and successfully released thousands of birds. Next to returning so many birds back to the air, another milestone in the Sanctuary's history was the breeding of birds in captivity. In 1975, "Pax" was born to permanently crippled parents. Since the birth of a pelican in captivity is a rare occurrence, this event was constantly monitored on a closed circuit television for 15 weeks. As far as research can determine, this was the first time that a pair of permanently crippled Brown Pelicans had successfully nested and reared offspring to the fledgling state. To date, the Sanctuary has had over 180 Brown Pelicans hatch from crippled parents and fly away to join other members of their species.

As Roger Tory Peterson, the great ornithologist and a frequent visitor to the Sanctuary, points out, "Birds are a unique indicator of environmental quality. What affects them can potentially affect us."

For further information:
Suncoast Seabird Sanctuary, Inc.
18328 Gulf Boulevard
Indian Shores, FL 34645
813-391-6211

Another U.S. resource that is inspiring is the Humane Society:

The Humane Society of the U.S.

"The Humane Society of the United States, a nonprofit organization, is devoted to making the world safe for animals through legal, educational, legislative, and investigative means. The HSUS is dedicated to speaking for animals, who cannot speak for themselves. We believe that humans have a moral obligation to protect other species with which they share the earth. Founded in 1954, The HSUS, with a constituency of more than a million persons, maintains several regional offices, an educational division, a team of investigators, legislative experts and an animal-control academy. "

For more information contact:
The Humane Society of the United States
2100 L Street, NW
Washington, DC 20037

I would also like to honor those I have discovered along the way who actively are participating in protecting and honoring the animal kingdom in many diverse ways. The list that is reprinted was compiled with the help of the World Goodwill Newsletter. I hope you will add to it and alert me of supportive organizations around the globe.

Following is a partial listing of worldwide cooperating organizations:

Australian and New Zealand Federation of Animal Societies—a grouping of over 50 animal societies in Australia and New Zealand. Active in a wide range of areas. ANZFAS, P.O. Box 1023, Collingwood, Victoria, Australia 3066.

Compassion in World Farming—campaigns for a fair deal for farm animals. CIWF, 20 Lavant Street, Petersfield, Hants. GU32 3EW. Similar work is done in the U.S. by Farm Animal Reform Movement, P.O. Box 70123, Washington, DC, USA 20088

Dr. Hadwen Trust for Humane Research—promotes development of valid techniques to substitute use of animals in medical and associated fields of research. Dr. Hadwen Trust, 6C Brand Street, Hitchin, Herts, U.K. SG5 1HX. Major work in the

U.S. done at Johns Hopkins Center for Alternatives to Animal Testing, Johns Hopkins School of Public Health, 615 North Wolfe Street, Baltimore, MD USA 21205.

Elefriends and Zoo Check, Cherry Tree Cottage, Coldharbour, Dorking Surrey UK RH5 6HA.

Environmental Investigation Agency–investigates abuses of wildlife and prepares highly effective international campaigns on such issues as the illegal ivory trade and the killing of pilot wales in the Danish Faroe Islands. EIA, Unit 32, 40 Bowling Green Lane, London, UK EC 1R 0NE.

Greenpeace International–national and international campaigns on a variety of issues for the protection and conservation of animals and their natural habitats. Greenpeace, 1436 U Street N.W., P.O. Box 96128, Washington, DC USA, 20090. Greenpeace International, Keizersgracht 176, 1016 DW Amsterdam, Netherlands.

Institut Juridique International pour la Portection des Animaux, 86 rue du Pas Saint Georges, 33000 Bordeaux, France.

International Union for Conservation of Nature and Natural Resources–a network of over 450 agencies and conservation organizations from more than 100 countries that plays a powerful role in leading the international community to act to conserve and protect endangered species of animals. IUCN, 1196 Gland, Switzerland.

World Society for the Protection of Animals–international campaigning organization with 360 member societies in over 60 countries. International HQ, WSPA, 106 Jermyn St., London, UK SW1Y 6EE; also regional centers at P.O. Box 190, 29 Perkins St., Boston, MA 02130 USA; Apartado Aereo 75002, Bogata, Columbia; 215 Lakeshore Boulevard East, Suite No. 113, Toronto, Canada M5A 3W9; No. 3 Totara Ave., New Lynne, Auckland 1232, New Zealand; P.O. Box 11733, 1001 GS Amsterdam Holland.

PURPOSES OF THE RADIANCE TECHNIQUE ASSOCIATION INTERNATIONAL, INC.

This corporation is a nonprofit public benefit corporation and is not organized for the private gain of any person. It is organized under the Nonprofit Public Benefit Corporation Law for charitable and public benefit purposes.

The specific purposes for which this corporation is organized are as follows:

1. To provide a non-voting international membership for both alumni of The Radiance Technique® and other interested supporters in order to promote, protect, enhance and expand the public understanding of and interest in The Radiance Technique®;

2. To provide for research and development projects and publishing projects pertaining to The Radiance Technique®; to promote through education, research and distribution of materials the widespread understanding of the science of universal energy, which is helpful, beneficent and benevolent to All Peoples; to explore and record the interaction of The Radiance Technique® with the living dynamic of people in their daily lives, with plants and with animals, and will all other living systems;

3. To maintain experiential data from the alumni of The Radiance Technique® as social research and service for this and future generations;

4. To provide for the ongoing education of the public regarding The Radiance Technique® and to publish on a continuous basis The Radiance Technique Journal, providing this publication as a service to members as well as distributing this publication as part of varied educational projects; to support the worldwide outreach of information through preparation and distribution of materials concerning The Radiance Technique® in written and audio/visual form;

5. To maintain an accurate historical recording of the history of The Radiance Technique® as a permanent archive and to provide and protect the continuance of archives;

6. To aid in Service to All Life Forms through the understanding of the Essential Unity and Oneness of All Life and the Inner-Relationship of the transcendental, Universal Energy Principle inherent in All Life;

114

7. To promote international understanding and cooperation in responsible group service for humanity with respect to initiating services and projects;

8. To cooperate with the other organizations and groups in Awareness, Honoring, Support, Interconnectedness, Interdependence, Nurturing and Understanding; in benevolent activities to further global humanness and peace; in the continuing development of true and honorable relationships and the expansion and development of Human Awareness and Service;

9. To hold and manage property and funds for charitable and public benefit purposes, including the assistance and support of charitable and public institutions, associations and undertakings;

10. The property of this Corporation is irrevocably dedicated to charitable and public benefit purposes and no part of the net income assets of this Corporation shall ever inure to the benefit of any director, officer or member thereof or to the benefit of any private person. Upon dissolution or winding up of this Corporation, its assets remaining after payment or provision for payment of all debts and liabilities of this Corporation shall be distributed to a non-profit fund, foundation or corporation which is organized for charitable or public benefit purposes and which has established for its tax-exempt status under Section 501(c)(3) of the Internal Revenue Code.

ADDRESSES FOR MORE INFORMATION

For information on The First and The Second Degree seminars and Authorized Instructors in your area; for information concerning membership in The Radiance Technique Association International, Inc. (T.R.T.A.I.), a nonprofit organization; for sending sharings to or inquiries about "The Radiance Technique Journal"; and for information on any books or pamphlets published on The Radiance Technique® to:

The Radiance Technique Association International, Inc.
P.O. Box 40570
St. Petersburg, Florida 33743-0570

For information on these books—*The 'Reiki' Factor in The Radiance Technique®*, by Barbara Ray, Ph.D.; *The Expanded Reference Manual of The Radiance Technique®*, by Barbara Ray, Ph.D., *The Radiance Technique® On The Job*, by Fred. W. Wright, Jr., and *The Radiance Technique® and the Animal Kingdom*, by Marvelle Lightfields:

Radiance Associates
P.O. Box 86425
St. Petersburg, Florida 33738*

*(Use this address also to send your sharings for future editions of *The Radiance Technique® and the Animal Kingdom*, addressed to Marvelle Lightfields. Please include the following statement which gives permission to print: "I hereby give permission to Dr. Barbara Ray and Marvelle Lightfields to use the information in the future editions of books on The Radiance Technique® and the Animal Kingdom"; and sign and date the statement.)

For information on all seminars for The Third Degree and beyond:

Coordinator
Radiance Stress Management International, Inc.
P.O. Box 86425
St. Petersburg, Florida 33738

SELECTED BIBLIOGRAPHY

Anthrozoos, a journal that explores the nature of interaction between humans, animals and the environment. Write to: University Press of New England, 17½ Lebanon St., Hanover, New Hampshire 03755.

Boone, J. Allen. Kinship With All Life. London and New York, Harper and Row, 1984

Lucis Trust, World Goodwill Newsletter, "Animal Rights, Expanding the Circle of Ethics and Compassion," 1190, No. 1. Write to: World Goodwill, 113 University Place 11th Floor, P.O. Box 722 Cooper Station, New York, N.Y. 10276, USA . . . or World Goodwill, 3 Whitehall Court Suite 54, London, England SW1A 2EF . . . or Bonne Volonte Mondiale, 1 Rue de Varembe (3e), Case Postale 31, 1211 Geneva 20, Switzerland.

Ray, Barbara. The Expanded Reference Manual of The Radiance Technique®
The 'Reiki' Factor in The Radiance Technique®
The Official Handbook of The Radiance Technique®
For information write to:
Radiance Associates
P.O. Box 86425
St. Petersburg, Florida 33738

The following is reprinted with permission from *The Radiance Technique Journal*, Winter 1988 edition.

REFLECTIONS

A part of a chant from the Tibetan Yoga dance of Non-Ego—a mandala (circle) of transformation and recognition.

"O Power from where the Sun does come,
Carrying the Spear of Great Compassion;
   Heya Hum Hum Hum

O Power Who rules where the Sun goes down
Carrying the Spear of Great Affection;
   Heya Hum Hum Hum

O Power Who dwells with the Giant of the Night
Carrying the Spear of Great Impartiality;
   Heya Hum Hum Hum

O Power of the Heavens above and the Earth below
O Great Power of the Center Who relates us all
And makes us relatives of all that is
Carrying the Spear of the Illumined Mind

Power of the Perfect Diamond standing on the prostrate heads
   of the Elements of Selfishness
Implanting in their four limbs the transformative Spears,
And in their Hearts the Spear of the Illumined One,
Transfixing them immovably:

Help us Recognize now the Elements of Hatred, Pride, Lust,
   Jealousy and Ignorance that lie within,
Now transferred and transmuted into the cardinal points of
   this Holy Circle
And Remain at Peace
   Heya Hum Hum Hum"

(from *MANDALA* by Jose and Miriam Arguelles)

ABOUT THE AUTHOR

Marvelle Lightfields

Marvelle Lightfields has studied to The Sixth Degree of The Radiance Technique® and is an Authorized Instructor who teaches The First Degree and The Second Degree. In addition, she has been personally trained by Dr. Barbara Ray as an Authorized Instructor for The Radiant Third Degree and The Third Degree for Personal Growth and Transformation (3A). She has continued to advance in her personal use of and her professional outreach with The Radiance Technique® which began in 1979. As a part of her longtime professional relationship with Dr. Ray, she assists Dr. Ray and serves as Senior Faculty member for the training and authorization of instructors of The First and The Second Degree. She travels and lectures in many countries and has traveled around the world representing the global outreach of The Radiance Technique Association International, Inc.

She is Chairperson of The Board of Directors of The Radiance Technique Association International, Inc. and serves as one of the Co-Editors of The Radiance Technique Journal, the worldwide magazine published by the Association.

Her education includes a B. A. in human development, combined with graduate study in psychological and transpersonal techniques. Her background is extensive and encompasses a career in the field of communications as well as counseling. She worked for more than 25 years in the television industry as a writer and producer, also helping to create the award-winning community project that established locally a national effort to bring fine literature, television and education together with the "Scripts in the Schools" project pioneered by CBS.

She has served as Director of Communications at the college level of administration and as a college instructor has taught hundreds of college students in journalism, creative writing, speech, communications, and interpersonal communications.

She maintains a practice in counseling and transpersonal psychology with students worldwide. Combining her background in business and her knowledge and skills in stress management, she conducts workshops for corporations and individuals instructing them in how to use The Radiance Technique® on the job and in varied situations of stress beyond the work environment.

Her interactions with animals and TRT began when she studied The First Degree and did hands-on with a dog and a cat in her household at the time. Over the years she has used TRT with animals of all kinds and in many different settings. She shares some of these experiences in the book. She wrote this book with the support of Dr. Ray and many radiant friends. She was inspired and helped very specifically by the three radiant and active cats that share her home. Two of them have golden eyes—Sunshine, a golden tabby, and Lotus Love, his sister, who is a calico. The third member of the household is Saqqara, a blue-eyed female blue-point Siamese.

Love all God's creation, the whole of it and every grain of sand. Love every leaf, every ray of God's light! Love the animals, love the plants, love everything. If you love everything, you will perceive the divine mystery in things. And once you have perceived it, you will begin to comprehend it ceaselessly more and more every day. And you will at last come to love the whole world with an abiding, universal love. Love the animals: God has given them the rudiments of thought and untroubled joy. Do not, therefor, trouble them, do not torture them, do not deprive them of their joy, do not go against God's intent.

Dostoevsky